CLOWNS

and Rats

Scare Me

CLOWNS

and Rats
Scare Me

Columns by
Cary Clack

·····································

Foreword by
Naomi Shihab Nye

Trinity University Press

SAN ANTONIO

For the Four Most Important Women in My Life
My mother, Jenny Clack
My grandmother, Annie Mae Clack
My late grandmother, Olga Thompson
My lady, Gloria Jean Treviño

And for my father, Charles Clack Jr.

Published by Trinity University Press
San Antonio, Texas 78212

Copyright © 2009 by Trinity University Press

This material is used by permission of the *San Antonio Express-News*.

Cover design by David Drummond
Book design by BookMatters, Berkeley

♾ The paper used in this publication meets the minimum requirements of
the American National Standard for Information Sciences—Permanence
of Paper for Printed Library Materials, ANSI z39.48-1992.

Library of Congress Cataloging-in-Publication Data
Clack, Cary.
    Clowns and rats scare me : columns /
by Cary Clack ; foreword by Naomi Shihab Nye.
        p.   cm.
    Summary: "A collection of the work of San Antonio Express-News columnist
Cary Clack, with a foreword by Naomi Shihab Nye. Clack covers national
issues such as terrorism, racism, and child abuse, but his keen sense of
humor often turns to the stuff of everyday life"—Provided by publisher.
    ISBN 978-1-59534-037-5 (pbk. : alk. paper)
    I. San Antonio Express-News. II. Title.
PN4874.C519A25   2009
814'.6—dc22   2009005220

Printed in Canada

13 12 11 10 09 — 5 4 3 2 1

Contents

....

Foreword   *Naomi Shihab Nye*   ix

Introduction   1

We need more people like 83-year-old Maury Maverick Jr.   10

Martha Stewart's similarities to Nelson Mandela are striking   12

Men, it's our duty as Texans to patronize Club Boom Boom   14

Talkin' 'bout my Temptations   16

The colossal battle against a gigantic snake   18

Don't put constraints on King's message   21

FCC says turkey breasts on TV must have dressing   24

Our votes honor the very brave   26

Even Moses protected confidentiality of his Source   28

That Voice, That Woman, the waiting   30

Not all "You People" in family   32

Here's the real dirt on Spurs   35

Shut out of my bailout   38

You won't believe—so stay tuned   41

Lying their behinds off   44

Clowns—they pop up everywhere   46

"Village" embraces brothers   49

Even simple lessons can be lost on well-meaning children   52

Target just couldn't have any more rude bell-ringers   54

If gravy's on ballot, will you vote then?   56

Give her credit for a worldwide movement   58

A politician who needs to shut up, not 'fess up   60

This mutt doesn't exactly inspire brotherly feelings   62

The speech a segregationist, and dad, should have made   64

Angel affirms a girl's faith   66

Jury duty: Bonding, respect, $6 a day   68

Valerie presses on through pain   71

Oh, baby, chest isn't best place 74

Saying goodbye to my Afro is a hairy proposition 76

Mind was Malcolm X's power 79

When T-Jeff meets Sally, again 82

Burying victims of another war 84

Coach's legacy is St. Gerard students 86

Nephew No. 6 can ask about anything—except women 88

Happy birthday to a brilliant thinker 90

Soldier's song ends in hymn 93

Bridging two cultures in San Antonio easy as a youth 96

Remember this name when you go to vote 99

Past disappears with ice house's demolition 102

2008 campaign will reveal America's racial tolerance 104

Bettas can be fine pets; just don't go on any trips 106

On the road to New York 108

Families of missing find bond amid hope 110

Heavens open up and weep over New York 112

New York chaplain dies doing what he was best at 114

Remembering the lost, seeking return to normal 116

Nuclear winter brings out the new boys of summer 118

Time, like terror, won't stand still 120

Writing last week's wrongs 122

Afghan immigrants forced to prove their citizenship 124

Profound message in simple greeting 126

Baseball helped take New Yorkers' minds off terror 128

Lifting every voice to honor those who fell 130

"We Shall Overcome" inspires another generation 132

A day to pay tribute and a day off 134

Let there be justice, joy on earth 136

Happy birthday to a legend 138

Amadou, it was never about you 141

If I were a spy—and I'm not saying I'm not 144

Picking up the pieces of shattered justice 147

Let's cheer for the underdog   152

Time to obsess about washing, not obsessing   154

San Antonians' goodness far exceeds caller's venom   156

An eerie reminder of Mississippi's plight   158

Family surrounded by past as they build a future   161

Hiding more than eggs on Easter   164

Man from Springfield a colossal individual   167

Obama's blackness irrelevant   170

Remembering beloved Kendra   172

Stand up to racism, Victoria   175

Name it, I've been called that   178

Coretta's march   180

Money talks, not Municipal Courts   183

Oh, St. Anthony, hear this fan's plea   186

Listen! They're playing their song   189

President should've asked us for more   192

Great joy can turn a city into a family   194

Get there one chat at a time   196

Something turned boy to killer   199

Paws-ing to savor my links to "Papa"   202

Losing a beloved family member in Vandross   204

Rededicating ourselves to a more perfect Union   206

Witness to a great American moment   208

Maury Maverick Jr. guided many "children"   212

Foreword

Cary Clack has a brilliant knack. More than one, actually. He writes in strong, surprising sentences, with an uncluttered, sparely elegant tone. There's something very classy and sleek about his voice. It can be wildly witty and then deliver a few well-placed knockout punches in the same column—simultaneously self-deprecating and savvy. A reader may roar with laughter and weep in almost weirdly quick succession. How does this guy do it?

Those of us lucky locals who have followed Clack's voice closely in the *San Antonio Express-News* for years know that, reading him, we will quickly be transported to somewhere meaningful—haunting, hilarious, informative, or intriguing. (It's no accident that he's long been one of the most popular masters of ceremonies in this city. People just want him to present . . . things, whatever they are.)

Whether Clack is considering turkey breasts, unexpected snakes inside his home, Dr. Martin Luther King Jr., intricate neighborhood issues, or the rights of children, readers are invited, quickly and deftly, into the circle. He wastes no time. In tougher-topic columns, he speaks with machete-sharpness, invoking the insanity of violence—say, the sorrow of too many lost children in one city in one year—and managing, in a very short space, to place all the deepest, desperate questions on the table. No matter how infuriating a topic, he is never sarcastic or mean. Sly understatement serves his style—as in his piece on Martha Stewart and Nelson Mandela.

Cary Clack always trusts his readers. He expects us to be awake, paying quick-witted attention to what goes on, placing crucial details into wider context. His voice wakes us up a little further every time. One feels, perhaps, an intensified power to contemplate after reading him—to put one and one together to find *story, legend, meaning, hope*. The vastly humane span of his considerations—his strong effort and ability to create so many different kinds of empathies, week after week, column after column—feels like one of those gifts people start hungering for. Here are depths and layers we can't live without.

So it's high time a book-length collection made Cary Clack's voice available to a grateful audience that wishes to hold more than one of his columns in hand at any given moment. We're so proud of him—and we want to give him to friends in other cities. Cheers to Trinity University Press for having the wisdom to make this book, and for talking Clack into doing it.

As much as many of us adore his funniest pieces (and are stunned to learn from his own introduction that humor was not his earliest intention or inclination), Clack may be the most moving when he speaks of heritage, history, and civil rights. What better time for his book to appear than 2009, the year the United States inaugurated President Barack Obama, himself a spectacularly gifted writer? Cary Clack's "Our Votes Honor the Very Brave," a 2006 column that ought to be required reading for every student in this country, ends, "I never vote alone."

A voice like Cary Clack's reminds us that in community, we're never alone at all. We are preciously, inextricably linked. We fortify one another.

Naomi Shihab Nye

Introduction

....

In the summer of 1995 I wrote a column about ethnic cleansing in Bosnia that generated an outraged letter to the editor saying I didn't know what I was talking about and calling me a "scribbling kid."

The many obscene and defamatory names some readers have thrown at me have made me want to either take a long hot shower with the most abrasive soap or register to carry a handgun for protection. But "scribbling kid" was so amusingly dismissive that when I read it I immediately laughed and embraced it. In journalism years I was a kid; I was a baby. I'd been writing my column for one year and one month and had just been hired full-time by the *San Antonio Express-News* the previous month.

Yet I was nearly 36—a latecomer to this blessed profession of journalism. That the "scribbling kid" back then, uncertain of my voice, insecure about my status and afraid of failing miserably, might eventually have enough columns, not to mention a few decent ones, to gather in a collection was something I never imagined.

Not a morning or evening passes in which I don't give thanks to God for the opportunity to earn a living as a writer, as a journalist who scribbles three columns a week and is given the option by my newspaper to write longer front-page pieces if I choose. This isn't a privilege I take for granted. I savor it and revel in the moments because I know it can be taken away from me at any time—which would really be embarrassing once this book comes out.

The truth is that growing up in San Antonio, Texas, I've always been a scribbling kid. My first grade teacher, Mrs. Wyatt, who was also my mother's first grade teacher, told my mother I would be a writer. I don't remember not writing. I wrote many stories and poems. Some of the stories were based on the ABC Tuesday night Movie of the Week, which often involved a murder mystery. I wrote and wrote, especially during Christmas break when I didn't have homework, but for some reason I stopped writing around the time I got to high school.

With one exception, I didn't resume writing until I was a junior in college, which meant I went about 11 years without writing, not counting a few notebook jottings and some of the worst song lyrics composed in the latter part of the 20th century. Those notebooks with the song lyrics are the only ones I've thrown away—at least I hope I threw them away.

The one exception was a Sunday op-ed piece I wrote for the *Express-News* in January 1983 advocating that Martin Luther King Jr.'s birthday be a national holiday. That was the first time I was published.

In 1984, my junior year in college, I began writing columns for a black East Side newspaper called the *San Antonio Snap.* I wrote about things happening in San Antonio and across the country, whatever interested me and came to mind. Because I was painfully shy and didn't want anyone to see me, I would drop my manuscript, which was sometimes handwritten, over the transom. I didn't get paid a dime, but the paper's publisher, Eugene Coleman, wanted me to give the column a title and asked to run it with my photo. Again, because I was too shy, I declined. Still he published every piece I submitted, and that allowed me to write and painfully try to discover my voice—if there was a voice to be discovered.

Around this time, the summer of 1984, I went to Atlanta as a scholar-intern at the Martin Luther King Jr. Center for Nonviolent Social Change. The piece I'd written on King, sent to the King Center at my grandmother's suggestion, got me an application and entry into the program, where students learn about nonviolence as a way of life and a tool for social change, and where they each work in their area of specialty.

Since I was calling myself a writer, the program's director, Lili Baxter, who became a mentor and close friend, placed me with Steve Klein, the center's communication director and Coretta Scott King's speechwriter. In that capacity I was able to write some of the commentaries Mrs. King delivered on CNN.

This is when the journalism bug bit me. But because I was a political science major at St. Mary's University with no experience except for my *Snap* columns and a couple of pieces in the school newspaper, there were no prospective employers to scratch my itch when I began sending out résumés and clips.

Because my only journalism experience was writing opinion pieces, I began to imagine myself as a columnist. Over nine years, beginning with my graduation from college in 1985, I mailed out dozens of packets to publications across the country and was rejected each time, usually without a reply. The *Express-News* rejected me three times. Thanks to a new black newspaper on the East Side, the *San Antonio Informer* owned by Tommy Moore, I was given another chance to write more columns and fatten my portfolio. But except for an op-ed piece published by the *New York Times* in November 1989 in an occasional series called Voices of a New Generation and a couple of pieces in the *Express-News* and the *San Antonio Light*, I wasn't having any success.

There were many years of unemployment, substitute teaching, unemployment, community organizing, unemployment, work at the King Center in Atlanta, and did I mention unemployment? Then along came Maury Maverick Jr., the legendary civil rights lawyer and Sunday *Express-News* columnist.

Maury was the son of the former San Antonio mayor and congressman Maury Maverick Sr. and the descendant of a historic family with deep roots in American history. One of his relatives signed the Texas Declaration of Independence. The word "maverick" comes from this family.

Anyone who knew Maury never knew anyone more devoted to freedom and social justice. He spent his entire life dedicated to their full realization. Apart from that, I was just one of hundreds of beneficiaries of his generosity and desire to see everyone get opportunities to succeed.

The pivotal point of my journalism career, the reason I have a career in journalism, is because when I met Maury in a typewriter shop and he learned that I wanted to break into journalism, he proceeded to open a door for me. I was always proud when he took credit for "discovering" me, and he was right.

He brought me to the attention of *Express-News* associate editorial page director Bob Richter, who asked me to write a piece for the op-ed page. After it ran in November 1993, I had lunch with Bob and the other associate editorial page director, Lynnell Burkett. Then I met the editorial page director, Sterlin Holmesly, who invited me to submit more pieces. Over the next few months he paid me $100 for each publication, until he offered me a column that began in June 1994. The column ran every other Wednesday. I was paid $100 per column, which meant that a good month for me was one with five Wednesdays so I could make $300.

In November of that year I asked Sterlin if they'd let me have the week between my columns; they wouldn't have to pay me for the extra columns. I wanted to write more, to get more than my foot into the newspaper and gain exposure and experience. That's how the column became weekly.

I was hired in March 1995 on a trial basis by the newsroom, was hired part time in April and was hired full time in June as a general assignment reporter. Four days a week I was paid by the newsroom as a reporter, and the other day I was paid by the op-ed page for my column. This will never happen again; reporters don't give their opinions in their stories, while a columnist is paid to give his or her opinion. The potential conflict would have been reporting "objectively" on a story I'd already given my opinion on as a column. This division of duties continued in 1996 when I became a features writer.

Usually columnists start off as reporters, but I was a columnist who became a reporter who wrote a column before becoming a full-time columnist. In 1998 I joined the editorial board as an editorial writer and columnist, and for the first time I became a full-time opinion writer. When I became a Metro columnist in 2000, I wrote a column three times a week, a workload—and I use that phrase lightly—that I still have in the paper's SA Life section.

One of my columnist colleagues at the *Express-News* once told me, "I envy the boundaries you have as a columnist, which are none." He's pretty much right. As a general interest columnist I've been allowed to write about all things that are of general interest to me and, I hope, to many of my readers. Not only have the editors given me the latitude to write about anything I want; they've also allowed me to experiment and use different styles and voices.

Another advantage a columnist has over a reporter is the freedom to be more creative in style and the way a piece is crafted. And going from a column every two weeks to a weekly column forced me to be creative. If I wanted to address an issue that other columnists had already written about or that was becoming stale, I had to write about it in a different way, approach it uniquely if I could. More and more, that way was with humor and satire.

In all the years I dreamed of being a full-time columnist, it never occurred to me that I'd use humor. I wanted to report, write and give my opinion on important issues and tell the stories of interesting people, not make people laugh. Humor wasn't something I consciously tried to do; it just happened. But I do remember that sometime in 1999 I began to feel I was about to burn out from writing too many columns and editorials about abused and murdered children, and the humor pieces became a bit more frequent. Soon I got to the point where, given a choice between coming at an issue seriously or humorously, I'd always go for the humor—if it was appropriate and I could make it work. That's the same route I take today.

While I believe that serious points can be better made with humor and satire, it's also all right to be funny simply for the sake of being funny. There's nothing wrong with just being silly and enjoying the laughs.

There are more columns in this book about race than there would probably be if I were a white columnist. I don't apologize for that. I've been forced to think about and deal with race all my life, even when I didn't know why. When I was an eight-year-old third-grader I wrote an essay titled "Black People Are People Too." I don't remember what was in the essay or why I wrote it, but something moved me to put what I was feeling on paper.

When I was first given the column I was conscious to not write about race too often. I didn't want to be pigeonholed as "the Black Columnist" who only writes about race. Now, because I've written so many columns about scores of other topics, I no longer worry about being pigeonholed; I've proven that I can and do write about more than race.

But that doesn't stop a segment of the population, each time I touch on something even tangentially related to race, from dragging out the tired and predictable accusation, "All you write about is race." I can go three months without writing about race, do it one time and still hear this. But I understand that it comes from those who are uncomfortable discussing race and even more uncomfortable when a black man discusses it.

It doesn't matter that each time I write about race it's to build bridges and not walls. For them it's proof of my own racism. It's taken me a while, but I now understand that it's their problem and not mine.

The question I'm asked more than any other about my job is where I get my ideas. The great advantage of being a general interest columnist with no boundaries is that I get them everywhere. It can be something in the news, something I saw or heard, the anniversary of a historic event, or some forgotten observation or comment I'd written in my notebook months earlier.

The antennae are always up, looking for anything I can carve 700 or more words out of. I try to not write too many of the same columns in a row, mixing the serious with the humorous and using different voices, styles and tones.

I write to the music that's in my mind, and some days the music decides what the topic will be. On mornings when I have no idea what I'm going to write about, I listen to the music. If it's something with a jazzy or hip-hop beat, that tells me to look for a topic I can have fun with. If the melody is slow, like a ballad, that means I'll write an essay that's more solemn and thoughtful.

Some weeks I have a cornucopia of ideas—so many that, like leftovers, I have to throw them away because they're more than I can consume. Other weeks I'm searching fallow ground hoping to find just three kernels of corn to tide me over until the next week.

I revisit certain themes and topics because of my interest but also sometimes because of necessity. Race is one topic, as are children, issues of social justice, nonviolence, Martin Luther King Jr., sports, music and the absurd.

Sifting through nearly 2,000 columns to select 84 for this book was more difficult than writing some of these pieces. I wouldn't say these are the best columns I've written, but they are representative of my work.

With two exceptions, the columns aren't organized in chronological or topical order. The first is the 13 columns I wrote from New York City after the attacks on Sept. 11, 2001. At 10:40 that morning, *Express-News* photographer Edward Ornelas and I were on the road to New York. We got into the city a little after 5 p.m. on the afternoon of Sept. 12. Soon after that I dictated my first column back to the paper while I sat on a shop stoop in Union Square Park. For the next 12 days I'd leave my hotel room in Times Square, walk the streets looking for stories and return to my room to write them. It was at once the most exhilarating and unsettling experience of my journalism career. The paper's decision to send me made me understand, for the first time, that management had a higher assessment of me and my abilities than I thought. All 13 of those columns appear together here in the order in which they ran.

The other exception is two columns on the man who made all of this possible for me, the great and irrepressible civil rights lawyer and columnist who opened the door for my entry onto the pages of the *Express-News*.

When Maury was going into the hospital in January 2003 I paid tribute to him by writing a column celebrating his birthday. When he died less than a month later, I wrote another tribute to him. Those two columns, in his honor, are the bookends to this collection.

Whenever I speak in schools I find myself marveling at my fortune. I tell students I have the opportunity not only to write for a living but to write about whatever I want and to give my opinions on the issues and people I write about.

Yep, this scribbling kid's been blessed.

CLOWNS

and Rats

Scare Me

We need more people
like 83-year-old Maury Maverick Jr.

1/4/2003

In late 1988, in a now defunct typewriter shop, I met Maury Maverick Jr. for the first time. Recognizing him from his Sunday column in the *Express-News*, I introduced myself.

The first thing he said to me was, "Black people need another Malcolm X."

I was struck by the force and sincerity of his comment. I learned later that anything involving social justice and politics is never far from his mind.

Friday was Maury's 82nd birthday. He moves slower, his eyes and ears are bad, and for years he's talked as if he expects the next day to be his last.

But the mind of this San Antonio original is still the sharp and searching instrument that has served him well in his careers—as state legislator, lawyer and journalist.

It's also served his city, state and nation. Maury is one of our great defenders of civil liberties and advocates for the dispossessed.

His eyesight may be weak, but his vision of a society truly rooted in the principles of the Bill of Rights and the simple precept that "God is love" remains clear and strong.

Most people know Maury from the Sunday column he's written for more than 20 years, a perch from which he writes about anything from the Constitution to nature.

If civil liberties have had no greater protector than Maury, the purple martin has had no greater friend than him. But before Maury did his fighting in his column, the former Marine combat veteran fought in the Texas House and the courtroom.

He was one of a few legislators in the early 1950s to stand up against the anti-Communist hysteria encroaching on the rights of American citizens.

Among his victories as a lawyer was the abolition of a law prohibiting professional boxing matches between blacks and whites. He also served as co-counsel with Gus Garcia and Carlos Cadena in the case in which the U.S. Supreme Court declared the exclusion of Mexican Americans from juries unconstitutional.

You can't take the stands and wage the battles and write the things that Maury has and be the belle of a lot of balls. There are those who don't like him, perhaps even hate him.

But there are many of us who consider him a treasure for the courage of his convictions, for his generosity, crustiness and humor.

"Maury is a lot smarter, tougher, more eloquent and kinder than you might think," says Bob Richter of the *Express-News* Austin Bureau, a longtime friend and former editor of Maury's work. "He might have made his mark as a lawmaker, civil rights lawyer and the son of a former mayor and congressman, but to me he's simply a good, kind friend, a patriot and one of the best read, most recognized journalists in this newspaper's more than 150-year history."

Were it not for Maury, I wouldn't have this column (which may give some people another reason to dislike him). He's the one who took some of my scribblings to the editorial board a few years ago, and that led to me getting a column on the op-ed page and eventually getting hired.

Yeah, we need another Malcolm X.

We also need a lot more Maury Maverick Jrs.

Thanks, Maury, and happy birthday.

Martha Stewart's similarities to Nelson Mandela are striking

7/21/2004

On Friday, Martha Stewart was sentenced to five months in prison, five months of home confinement and two years of supervised probation for obstructing a federal securities investigation. That night, in an interview with ABC's Barbara Walters, she imprecisely invoked the name of Nelson Mandela when asked about doing prison time. "I'm going to have to face it and take it and do it and get it over with," Stewart said. "And there are many other people that have gone to prison. Look at Nelson Mandela. Twenty-seven years in prison." Scene: Five months after Stewart went into prison, it's the day of her release.

"Good morning and welcome to *Good Morning Connecticut.* I'm Bob Blank, and this is my co-host Janice Filler. Along with thousands of media and spectators, we are gathered outside the Federal Correctional Institution in Danbury, Conn., where, today, after five long months, Martha Stewart will finally be released from prison. Janice, many of us never thought we'd live to see this historic day."

"Historic is right, Bob. Because she has been out of the public eye for so long, Martha Stewart is simply a myth to many of us, a larger-than-life figure we only know through film footage. The 63-year-old Stewart was 63 years old when her incarceration began, so no telling how much she has changed."

"Well, one way she has changed is that because of her admiration for Nelson Mandela, she will have her name legally changed to Martha Mandela Stewart."

"Bob, the similarities are striking. After Mandela was convicted he said, 'I have fought against white domination and I have fought against black domination. I have cherished the ideal of a democratic and free society in which all persons live together in harmony and with equal opportunities. It is an ideal which I hope to live for and to achieve. But if need be, it is an ideal for which I am prepared to die.' "

"And Janice, after Stewart was convicted she uttered these equally eloquent words: 'Perhaps all of you out there can continue to show your support by subscribing to our magazine, by buying our products, by encouraging our advertisers to come back in full force to our magazines.' Those are powerful words, Janice."

"Indeed. While Stewart has yet to duplicate Mandela's winning of the Nobel Peace Prize, she did send him a lengthy letter on what polish he can use to keep that medal looking as new and shiny as the day he received it."

"Yes, the now famous Letter from a Connecticut Minimum Security Prison."

"Bob, isn't there already a Martha Mandela? The one who sang 'Dancing in the Streets'?"

"That was Martha Reeves and the Vandellas, Janice, but there's DANCING IN THE STREETS now because Martha Stewart is walking out of the prison gates! There she is, hand in hand with her daughter and magazine subscriptions to pass out to her cheering fans!"

"Alexis is her daughter's name, Bob. The 39-year-old was just 39 years old when her mother went into prison."

"Janice, for a woman who has been locked up for five months, Stewart is looking good."

"She certainly is. And listen to her appreciative fans. Here's one. Sir, this is a great day. Do you think Stewart's prison sentence was excessive?"

"No, I think five months is just right for white-collar crime."

"And your name, sir?"

"Ken Lay."

Men, it's our duty as Texans to patronize Club Boom Boom

4/12/2004

A new plan unveiled by Gov. Rick Perry to increase public school funding includes a proposal for a $5 admission fee at topless bars and other "live entertainment" venues.

Stripped down to raw numbers, the proposition titillates with the promise of raising $45 million in both 2006 and 2007. At $5 per entry into a strip club, that means Texans are expected to visit these places 9 million times a year.

Nine million annual visits to strip clubs. NINE MILLION!

This is outrageous. This is embarrassing. This is appalling.

Men, we can do better.

Fate, circumstances, budgetary shortfalls and a concern for children and the state's future have now made it clear that men have an obligation to visit strip cubs more often.

With our eyes we can improve schoolchildren's minds. We can help kids learn to read *Little Red Riding Hood* by paying an additional $5 to watch Little "Miss Wow!" Red take off her riding hood.

Who would have thought that those visits to Club Boom Boom would someday be seen as an act of civic responsibility?

I admit to not being experienced in traveling the strip club circuit. The closest for me was the hootchie-cootchie dancer at Maury Maverick Jr.'s funeral that he'd requested. And if Maury knew he could have charged for that dance, with the proceeds going to education, we might have raised $1,500 that day.

I've only been to one strip club, and that was at the insistence of two female friends in Brownsville. Unfortunately, the night I went was the one night this particular club featured male strippers. (Did I mention I was with two women?)

I hung out near the bar in the back with other guys who'd picked the wrong night to drop in. We talked about girlfriends, hunting, brawling and surgeries we'd gone through without anesthesia, all the while hoping no one we knew would recognize us. (I know I mentioned that I was there with two women, but did I do it in a tough, masculine kind of way?)

But that faux pas proves that the financial foundation for educating Texas' children isn't a burden only to be carried by men ogling women at strip clubs. It's a load that can, and must, be carried also by women ogling men at strip clubs.

What a beautiful way of illustrating how the education of our children, and seeing naked people to pay for that education, cuts across gender lines. When it comes to stripping for education, all of us can play a part.

College coeds who dance at these clubs to help pay their way through school can now dance knowing that they're dancing and stripping not only for themselves but for that fourth-grader who wants to be an astrophysicist.

Given the propensity multimillionaire athletes have for visiting strip clubs, there are some professional teams that will be able to finance entire school districts by themselves.

From now on, husbands who want to visit a club can simply tell their wives, "Honey, me and the boys are going out to build a school."

The $5 admission fee to strip clubs to finance public education is an ingenious way to replace the current "Robin Hood" funding system.

Which reminds me, tonight at Club Oh Yeah, Robin "Bambi" Hood will be the featured performer in "Lap Dances for Laptops Night."

It's all about the children.

Talkin' 'bout my Temptations

....

5/5/2006

On a cold January night in 1964, five young men walked down a Detroit street and into immortality.

Their names were Otis Williams, Melvin Franklin, Paul Williams, Eddie Kendricks and David Ruffin, who was the newest member of the Temptations.

They were walking to the studio where, that night, they would record "The Way You Do the Things You Do," the first of the hit records that would establish the Motown group as the greatest vocal group of all time.

As the group strolled, Otis, the founder and leader, dropped back and watched his best friends walk ahead until he could no longer hear their footsteps.

Forty-one years later, he still remembers this scene, which he wrote about in his autobiography. "I knew these were the five God was going to let step into history," Williams said via telephone from his home in Los Angeles.

The 65-year-old Williams is the last surviving original member of the Temptations. None of the others lived past the age of 52.

There have been many personnel changes in the group, which continues to record and perform. Their 1998 album, *Phoenix Rising*, was their biggest-selling album. Tonight the Temptations will perform at the Westin La Cantera to benefit the Juvenile Diabetes Research Foundation.

But the quintet of Otis, Melvin, Paul, Eddie and David was the template for class, five-part harmonies, mesmerizing choreography and stylish attire. Their unique sound made them legends.

"There will never be anything like the original Temptations," says the Texas-born Williams. "On stage you could feel the magic. It was uniquely special."

Now there's just him.

"It's hard to put into words, but I never imagined this," he says. "We grew up together and had fun. I think about them often. I'm looking at their pictures on the wall as I talk to you and they're all here—and they're all gone."

If only one must remain, it's fitting that it's the one who first saw the group's potential for greatness. When there were problems, Motown founder Berry Gordy Jr. would demand: "Get me Otis! Get me Otis!"

This week, the Temptations severed their relationship with Motown.

"It's too corporate," Williams says. "It hasn't been the same since Berry sold it. They ought to close it down and let it become a catalog company."

Williams doesn't plan on closing the Temptations down anytime soon. "I'm going to ride the hair off of this horse," he laughs. "I'm still having fun."

But when he stops performing, should the group continue? Williams isn't sure.

"I wonder if people will accept the group if I'm not there," he says. "People expect to see me."

Melvin, Paul, Eddie and David have walked ahead of Otis into eternity, their footsteps long silenced. But each time he takes the stage, he breathes life into memories and reminds us of their magical voices and presence and of those incredible songs, including "My Girl," which Williams calls timeless.

"It's a blessing to have been able to survive," he says.

It's our blessing to still have Otis Williams with us in this month of May.

The colossal battle
against a gigantic snake

7/3/2008

I don't have many fears other than being unemployed, homeless, friendless, rejected by my family, covered with honey and tied to a bed of fire ants, the flying monkeys from *The Wizard of Oz*, squash, computer paper, ghosts named Maggie, falling out of the space shuttle right before it leaves the Earth's atmosphere, licorice, elves, lawnmowers, unwashed hands, waking hours and being romantically linked to Madonna and Alex Rodriguez.

Other than that I'm a normal, stable, laid-back kind of guy.

The only two things that, since childhood, have given me the creepy chills are clowns and rats. I can't explain the clown thing except for too many afternoons watching the Joker on *Batman*, which is why I also have a fear of Cesar Romero. Even though he's been dead several years, I'm afraid he'll come back as a ghost named Maggie offering me licorice.

A couple of years ago, *Express-News* TV critic Jeanne Jakle, knowing of this fear, showed up at my birthday party wearing a clown mask. Maybe it's only in my mind, but since our offices are next to each other, I swear I hear her playing circus music to taunt me.

Growing up in a house where I would hear rats in the walls near my bed or rummaging through the kitchen and where I would have to remove their carcasses from bloody traps (sorry if you're eating while reading this), I really have a problem with rats. Mice, not quite so much, but it's close.

One morning a couple of months ago, while writing at home, I noticed my two cats, Sinatra and Raskolnikov, preoccupied with something. When I got up to look I was surprised to hear a woman's voice shriek and say, "EEE, a mouse!" I was really surprised to realize that the voice had come from my mouth.

The area where the Clack Cave is secretly ensconced is home to many a critter and varmint, including a coyote or two that, after 10 p.m., forage in my backyard for food. There are also snakes of varying degrees of size and venom.

Two weeks ago I walked into my kitchen and saw Sinatra eyeing a foot-long snake that had entered through the garage. Thinking that Sinatra had already performed his watch-cat duties, I wrapped the snake in newspaper—AFTER I'D READ THE NEWSPAPER AND CUT OUT THE MANY IMPORTANT STORIES THAT EACH NEWSPAPER CARRIES EVERY DAY BECAUSE THE PRIMARY PURPOSE OF NEWSPAPERS IS TO BE READ AND NOT TO WRAP UP FISH AND SNAKES— put it in a garbage bag and deposited it in the kitchen trash.

When I returned home a few hours later, the garbage bag was on the floor and the 2-foot-long snake was coiled in a corner of my dining room. Nudging it and seeing that it still had a little life in it, I swept it into a dustpan, covered it with a broom and was walking to the front door when the 4-foot-long snake started slithering wildly and fell out of the dustpan and onto the carpet.

At this point it occurred to me that I should be a little more afraid of the snake because I didn't know if it was poisonous. In the second that thought crossed my mind and I looked away, the snake had disappeared into one of four rooms, one of which was my bedroom.

Not being able to find it, I got on the Internet and Googled "How to identify venomous snakes." One site actually said, "Nonvenomous snakes usually have a round pupil in the eye."

Do you know how close you have to get to a snake to see if it has a round pupil in the eye? So close that if it doesn't have a round pupil it's too late.

The same site said the venomous snakes "have an elliptical

pupil like a cat's eye. It looks like a small slit in the middle of the eye."

That helped a lot because then all I had to do was ask my cat, "Sinatra, did that snake have an elliptical pupil like yours?" To which he would answer, "Couldn't tell, boss, but I know they weren't blue and pretty like mine."

After a while, I saw the 9-foot-long snake in my bathroom. The smart thing to do was to take something and bash or cut it. I'm not smart, I'm Cary, and having just cleaned my bathroom floor I didn't want to stain it with snake blood. So I reached for a can of ant and roach spray that seemed to have the effect steroids have on baseball players—it made the snake stronger.

So I reached for the wasp spray, and it knocked that sucker out. Not only did it kill the snake; it also removed my fear of wasps invading my bathroom.

After dragging the anaconda out of the bathroom, I wrapped it in AN OUT-OF-TOWN NEWSPAPER, a bookstore bag and two garbage bags, hit it a couple of times with a hammer and set it out in the sun.

That's how I did battle with a gargantuan snake and saved San Antonio from its venomous bite. But if it had been a rat, I'd still be running to Atlanta and y'all would have to fend for yourselves.

Don't put constraints
on King's message

1/14/2007

A mystery shadows San Antonio's annual Martin Luther King Jr. March. It's a mystery that deepens each year with each step taken by the tens of thousands of marchers. It's one that's not only pondered by San Antonians but by others across the country. Last week at an Optimist Club meeting, I was asked by motivational speaker and "Mr. Optimist" Ron Graves how I would answer the question he's often asked in his travels, and that's how San Antonio, a city with a small African American population, each year has the biggest King holiday march?

Cancel the calls to Sherlock Holmes and Kojak, because there is no mystery. Turn the question around and ask why shouldn't a city with a small African American population, such as San Antonio, have the largest march?

The assumption that gives birth to the mystery of this city's huge turnout is that cities with large black populations should have the largest turnouts.

The assumption is false because it narrowly defines King as a black man speaking out and fighting only for blacks.

Of course, King was an African American who was nurtured in the African American church and who became the face and voice of the struggle of African Americans, one of this nation's largest disenfranchised groups for much of its history. He was a drum major for justice, wielding a baton of nonviolence, who led a parade of conscience through the streets and soul of America.

But the genius of King was that his was a ministry of inclusion, and he advocated for ideals enshrined in the Declaration of Independence and Constitution, ideals of freedom, justice and human treatment that people everywhere and in any time aspire to.

The scope of King's vision and mission and the vitality of the philosophy of nonviolence he lived and espoused are too broad for him to be limited by the straitjacket titles of "black" or "civil rights" leader.

These definitions are too small for a man who is a world historical figure and, arguably, the most influential American of the 20th century when measured by his impact on freedom movements throughout the world.

More than 15 years ago, when Václav Havel, the playwright turned dissident turned president of the Czech Republic, met Shen Tong, one of the Chinese student leaders of the Tiananmen Square rebellion, they spent most of their time discussing King's influence on their lives.

The irony is that little attention, except fleetingly, at this time of year, is given to the messages of nonviolence and love that make King a leader who transcends time and boundaries. The best way to honor and continue King's legacies would be for communities, schools, religious institutions, neighborhood associations, families and corporations to initiate programs in which the history and philosophy of nonviolence is taught and discussed.

We need programs that would teach that nonviolence isn't simply the absence of physical violence but the presence of justice; that would teach that nonviolence isn't about ego, personal gain, bearing false witness or humiliating and demonizing others; that would teach that nonviolence is love in action and that as long as there is suffering and injustice somewhere, we have an obligation to do what we can to help.

We're all imperfect creatures trying to do better and be better, and King believed we all had the capacity to have "a heart full of grace. A soul generated by love." The essence of nonviolence is the way we treat each other.

Very few people truly understand King, or we'd do better at embracing nonviolence and trying to love a little bit more. But if San Antonio, again on Monday, has the largest King holiday march in the nation, it's no mystery.

It just means this city understands that King belongs to all of us.

FCC says turkey breasts
on TV must have dressing

11/24/2004

Responding to inappropriate images on television and bowing to a public disgusted with lax moral standards, the Federal Communications Commission has banned television commercials advertising turkey breasts.

"We want Americans to know that we're serious about cleaning up television and making it more family-friendly," explained FCC spokesman Nitt Picking. "We've been flooded with letters from parents complaining that while watching *CSI: Miami* with their children they were shocked when up popped a commercial showing an exposed, carved turkey breast on a dining room table being lustfully gawked at by adults and children. Children!"

This year has seen a loosening of standards on network television. It began with controversy over Janet Jackson's exposed breast at the Super Bowl halftime show and is ending with more outrage over *Desperate Housewives* co-star Nicollette Sheridan dropping her towel and exposing her back in a pre-Monday Night Football skit with the Philadelphia Eagles' Terrell Owens.

"Our country is sliding down the slippery slope of Nicollette Sheridan's bare back into the Sodom and Gomorrah of the constant showing of nude turkey breasts," Picking said. "Maybe we can't prevent children from being exposed to this filth in the poultry sections of grocery stores—and if I had my way turkey breasts couldn't leave the store unless they were wrapped in brown paper—but we can at least keep it off of our public airwaves."

Picking was asked about the potential harm to the turkey

industry by forbidding the breasts to be shown on commercials advertising turkey.

"You can still show every other part of the turkey's anatomy on television," he said. "Drumsticks, thighs, giblets—all of that is fine and clean. We just can't allow the most sexually suggestive of a turkey's body parts to be shamelessly flaunted. Just last night, while watching *Fear Factor* with my 7-year-old son, a commercial showed a platter of sliced turkey breast with steam rising from the turkey. My son saw that and said, 'Dad, that turkey is hot!' Call me old-fashioned, but 7-year-old boys should not be titillated over naked turkey breasts. Besides, the public airwaves are not the place to promote immoral animals with multiple spouses."

Reached in Turkey Cove, Texas, Mel Mel Gobbler, president of the South Texas Turkey Association, had mixed reactions to the FCC's new rule.

"First, in this most violent of seasons for my birds, when turkeys are slaughtered for the eating pleasures of people, I certainly hope that the FCC's banning of turkey breast commercials on television will reduce our appeal to consumers," said Gobbler. "We want to live in peace and not be in pieces on Thanksgiving."

Gobbler repeated his long-held assertion that serving turkeys at the first Thanksgiving in Plymouth was a mistake.

"Our first four martyrs to your holiday completely misunderstood the invitation," said Gobbler. "They thought they were going there to be served as guests, not served as the meal."

But Gobbler was upset with the FCC spokesman's contention that turkeys are immoral animals.

"Male turkeys are polygamous but are very family-oriented," he said. "I'm loyal to all 67 of my families."

I wish a safe and happy Thanksgiving to each of you

Our votes honor the very brave

10/24/2006

On my way to the voting booth on Monday morning, I high-fived Martin Luther King Jr., shook hands with the Rev. James Reeb and hugged Fannie Lou Hamer.

As I studied the ballot, I slapped the backs of civil rights workers Michael Schwerner, James Chaney and Andrew Goodman.

After I marked my electoral choices, I sent appreciative thoughts to John Lewis in Atlanta and tipped my hat to LBJ and Sen. Everett Dirksen.

On the first day of early voting I cast my ballot without incident because the most dangerous and serious incidents had preceded me exercising my civic obligation and right.

There was no excuse not to vote because the excuses had been washed away with blood and tears. No barriers blocked my path because they'd been removed by the activism of folks like King, Reeb and Hamer and the legislative work of politicians like Johnson and Dirksen.

So I didn't have to maneuver my way past snarling dogs and state troopers to get inside the building, and the registrars didn't tell me to pay a poll tax or pass some arcane literacy test before letting me vote—which I did, knowing I had no fear of my employer punishing me for doing so.

This year's midterm elections are the 40th anniversary of the first midterm elections held after the passage of the 1965 Voting Rights Act, the legislative crown jewel of the civil rights movement. It removed the most obvious and egregious obstacles to voting.

The struggle, suffering and loss of life that led to that legislation isn't from the dusty and yellowed pages of our national history book, but from pages so fresh that the ink can still be smelled. It's recent enough to have happened during the lifetimes of a significant segment of living Americans, many who bear the scars yet carry the triumphant mantle of that struggle.

Each time I go to vote, I think of Bloody Sunday, March 7, 1965, when John Lewis, now a congressman, led 600 demonstrators in an attempt to cross the Edmund Pettus Bridge in Selma; they were turned back and beaten by Alabama state troopers.

I think of Bloody Sunday, a crucial date in the Selma campaign that led to eventual passage of the Voting Rights Act, and I can never take voting for granted.

Adding early voting to Election Day means that we have 13 days to vote. Thirteen. Not too long ago, people were getting their heads busted trying to simply register for one day of voting, and we have 13 days that millions of eligible voters will let pass them by without going to the polls.

There are no Edmund Pettus Bridges blocked by armed lawmen keeping us from voting. Yes, shenanigans are still being played to intimidate and mislead people, and electronic voting is an electoral catastrophe waiting to happen, but that's all the more reason to be vigilant and safeguard everyone's right to vote and exercise our own.

There's much about our political system—mostly, the people we allow to control it—that breeds cynicism and disheartens people enough to keep them from voting. But when we don't vote the cynics win, and voting can be a powerful antidote to cynicism. We vote for ourselves and the generations that will follow, and we vote for those who made it possible.

Jimmy Lee Jackson of Meridian, Miss., and Viola Liuzzo of Detroit, Mich., were two of the martyrs of the Selma campaign On Monday morning, I took them with me into the voter's booth.

I never vote alone.

Even Moses protected confidentiality of his Source

7/18/2005

The rights of journalists to protect their sources has dominated the news with the controversy surrounding New York Times *reporter Judith Miller and* Time *magazine reporter Matthew Cooper and the naming of a CIA agent. This case offers us a chance to look back to when Moses was forced to appear before a grand jury.*

"Please state your name for the record."

"Moses."

"And your last name?"

"That's it. Just Moses."

"And Mr. Moses—"

"Sir, Moses is my first and only name."

"Excuse me. Would you like a gourd of water?"

"I'm fine. I have a rock and my staff."

"Moses, what is your occupation?"

"Well, I do a bit of everything. I'm a religious leader, political organizer, lawmaker, military strategist, emancipator, journalist."

"Seems like you have a hard time holding down a job. Now, Moses, it's that last occupation of yours that brings us here together. Why are you considered the greatest living reporter?"

"That's not how I would ever refer to myself, but I guess people call me that because I got the interview of the ages when I journeyed up to Mount Sinai."

"And when you—Will someone please get these frogs out of here? Where did they come from? And when you journeyed up to Mount Sinai, what did you come down with?"

"Two tablets."

"And what was on those two tablets?"

"The Ten Commandments. Actually, there were 42 Commandments, but an editor got a hold of them. Ha ha. Just kidding. A little Old Testament journalism humor."

"Moses, who was the source for the Ten Commandments?"

"Huh?"

"Who— Now where in Hades did these flies come from? Who was the source that tipped you off to the Ten Commandments?"

"Sir, for the time being, until my source gives me permission to do so, I will not and cannot reveal my source."

"Moses, you do— Where have these gnats come from? Moses, you do understand that by not releasing the name of your source for the Ten Commandments, you risk imprisonment?"

"Sir, until told otherwise, I've pledged confidentiality to my source. You might say that we have a covenant."

"Is it true that your code name for your source is Burning Bush?"

"No, it's not."

"What about reports that you would regularly meet with your source behind a cloud on Mount Sinai? And what is that noise outside?"

"Sir, I will not comment on where I spoke with my source. And I believe it's hailing outside."

"My God, frogs, gnats, flies and hail. You'd think someone was trying to send us a message."

"My God, indeed, sir. One would think that."

"OK, Moses, we're not playing. Who was your confidential source for the Ten Commandments?"

"Sir, I'll wander 40 years through a desert before telling you that. And you have a locust in your beard."

Because his source did decide to reveal Himself, Moses avoided prison and retired from journalism knowing he could never share with readers a more important line than "Thou shalt not kill."

That Voice,
That Woman, the waiting
....

1/19/1996

She kept me waiting. Women will do that to a man, and to a boy. But Barbara Jordan kept me waiting.

The spell was first cast with That Voice, which rolled richly with the wisdom of Mother Earth and the cadences of 300 years of black Baptist preaching.

It awakened the slumber of a child dozing in front of the television set during those endless Watergate hearings when it intoned: "My faith in the Constitution is whole. It is complete. It is total." I had no idea what she meant, but I knew she was special.

Then came the summer night in 1976 that would start my waiting, when she stood at the podium in Madison Square Garden at the Democratic National Convention and declared: "There is something special about tonight . . . I, Barbara Jordan, am the keynote speaker."

Another awakening. This time, of a teenager's budding political consciousness.

So I waited for the summer night when she would stand at the podium and say: "I, Barbara Jordan, accept the nomination for president of the United States."

Or the wintry afternoon when she would pledge: "I, Barbara Jordan, do solemnly swear . . ." in taking her oath for the presidency.

It seemed outrageous yet possible: a black woman as president. Not that I doubted the ability of black women. Being raised by a mother and two grandmothers taught me about the strength and possibility of black women.

But seeing Jordan bathed in the adulation of thousands of delegates made it seem within reach. Surely she would reach for it.

But she kept me waiting.

Like her namesake, Michael, would do years later, Jordan left the arena of elected office while at the top of her game. But unlike the basketball star, this virtuoso of public life didn't return.

Though the frailty of her body couldn't sustain the life of a politician, the power of her intellect and the quality of her character made her an invaluable public servant.

As a professor at the Lyndon B. Johnson School of Public Affairs at the University of Texas, Jordan shaped the minds, and more importantly the values, of a future generation of public officials.

How well she taught is indisputable. How well they learned will be judged by their careers.

She even taught those of us who never had the opportunity to take any of her courses. As much as anyone else, it was Barbara Jordan who taught me the power of language, of using the written and spoken word to move and entertain.

She helped me learn that in the battle of ideas and the bolstering of ideals, there are no more effective weapons than the marshaling of words in a distinctive and honest voice.

She was magnificent in her dignity, integrity and talent. A symbol of individual talent used for the public good.

But she kept me waiting.

Not all "You People" in family

"White people have all the brains in this country. You people don't have any manners. . . . You people need to get educated and learn to speak English" (female caller, ExpressLine, Jan. 4).

I wrapped myself in these warm sentiments (which were politely and articulately expressed) as I journeyed here to scour the frozen tundra for the legendary "You People."

The You People are known to inhabit dark and unexplored hinterlands. While they have been seen most prominently among people of Negroid descent, there have been sightings of them among various species.

For years, scientists and explorers have marveled at the adaptability of You People and their ability to melt into other groups.

My personal interest in You People stems from an incident at a swimming pool when I was 9 years old and in a summer program at the YMCA.

Before going into the pool, all of us kids (Little People) lined up so that the program director, Bob, could put suntan lotion on us. When it was my turn, Bob gave me a puzzled look.

"I didn't think You People used suntan lotion," he said.

Instinctively, I sensed what he meant. As I looked around the Alamo Heights pool, I realized that if I was a You People, there weren't a lot of You People swimming.

The discovery that the blood of You People flowed in my veins was an exciting time for me. It, more than anything else, set me on my distinguished scientific career.

On that particular day of childhood revelation, I raced home to tell my family.

"Hey, y'all," I shouted. "We're a You People."

"We know," they answered. "But which part of us?"

I knew what they meant. My family and genes are made up of a lot of You People: African Americans, Mexican Americans, Puerto Ricans, Haitians, Italians and, yes, Anglos.

One of my great-great-grandfathers was a French Jew. Another one was an Anglo slaveowner. A great-great-uncle was a ruffian who was killed in a gunfight with Wild Bill Hickok in Abilene, Kan. (Uncle Phil was the "white sheep of the family.")

African Americans in my family have skin tones ranging from white to black. Both of my grandmothers could have passed for white (which means, dear caller, when you're talking to Your People about You People, you may actually be talking to a You People).

My family looks like M&M candies minus the green ones and those new blue ones.

Apparently, great-great-Grandpa T. had a remarkable tolerance for You People during the late nights he slipped out to the slave quarters when the Mrs. was asleep.

See, one of the first things I discovered in my search for You People is that they may not be a pure breed. My research and studies show that it takes a lot of Other People to make You People.

So which You People are we? Which roots? Alex Haley had it easy. He only had to go to Africa. My travels have taken me all over the world.

Here, in the heartland of the United States of You People, my search is once again proving futile.

I have slogged through the snow and ice of this region's dairies, careful not to step on inebriated Green Bay Packer fans who lie facedown in the snow. I believe they may be a new breed of You People, but they're too young to be of any use to me.

Perhaps I'll have to face the reality that You People don't exist and that lineage is false. Maybe I'll have to study the theory that the You People are a myth created by a species called the "incredibous ignoramus." But I've been searching too long to stop now. The You People are out there somewhere, and I will find them, goshdarnit.

And I won't stop there. After I've discovered the You People, I will begin my search for their equally legendary cousins: Those People.

Here's the real dirt on Spurs

···

6/7/2007

"Welcome to *NBA Jive*. I'm your host, Hoops Baller. Tonight's question: How dirty are the San Antonio Spurs? It wasn't so long ago that the Spurs were known as one of the classiest organizations, with some of the nicest players in all of sports. But overnight during the playoff series against the Phoenix Suns, they transformed from a team some labeled soft into one that many people outside of the Alamo City are calling the dirtiest team in the NBA. Here to help us discuss this is Spurs spokesman Hacksaw Bruiser. Mr. Bruiser, are the Spurs the dirtiest team in the NBA?"

"Oh, yeah. We're not just dirty; we're filthy and nasty. Dirt, sand, mud, gravel, lava, that's us."

"So the Spurs don't mind being known as the NBA's new bad boys?"

"Nah, because we're bad, real bad. I hope you had a good flight down here, Hoops."

"I did. But I'm surprised because I don't look at your team like that and I assumed that the organization and city would resent this new label."

"The Spurs are gangsters, and gangsters don't give a darn what people think about them. And if there's anything we can do to help you while you're in San Antonio, Hoops, don't hesitate to ask. Look, we admit that the negative things people were saying about us took us aback. We figured them to be the same crack smokers who call us boring. How can any team with Tony Parker, who's faster than a rumor, or Manu Ginobili, a human grenade rolling around the court waiting to explode, be boring? But when we realized that being called dirty was giving us a mystique and might intimidate our opponents, we decided to embrace the inner thug in each of us."

"So your real name isn't Hacksaw Bruiser?"

"Ah, no, it's Seymour Milton Culpepper IV. But you better call me Hacksaw or Mr. Bruiser! Don't disrespect me, Hoops, or I will do something bad to you because we're, you know, real bad!"

"OK, Hacksaw."

"I didn't mean to raise my voice at you, Hoops. Please forgive me."

"So just how dirty are the Spurs?"

"Oh, man. Real dirty, no respect for rules or anyone."

"Give me an—ouch! Did you just pinch me?"

"See there, Hoops. When you least expect it. We bring the pain, baby, the Spurs bring the pain . . . I didn't hurt you, did I?"

"I'm skeptical, Hacksaw. I find it hard to believe that there's anything dirty or sinister about the Spurs. Come on, your superstar, the face of your franchise, is a calm and gentle giant."

"Tim Duncan killed six people in the Virgin Islands before he was 16, Hoops! You didn't know that, did you? Fabricio Oberto was an assassin for the Argentine government for four years! Tony's the main man in the Longoria Syndicate. We hurt people, Hoops! We hurt people and love it. By the way, here are some lifetime passes to SeaWorld and Fiesta Texas for your children."

"Thanks. And Coach Popovich tolerates this?"

"Man, Pop is our lead gangster. Sometimes he'll gather the team around and say, 'Fellows, no practice today. We're just going to hang out and be thuggish today and do thug things.'"

"Pop says that?"

"Yep."

"And what are some of the thuggish things the team does?"

"Well, you know those allegations about Michael Vick?"

"The Spurs are into pit bull fighting?"

"No, no. Panda bears."

"What?"

"Panda bear fighting. Most of the guys own panda bears, so we get together, put soft and fluffy pillows on the paws of the bears and let them go at it."

"How dirty are you going to be toward LeBron?"

"Real dirty. The fans are going to help us mess that kid up. You know how he spells his name with a capital 'B'?"

"Yes."

"Well. We're going to have posters spelling it with a small 'b.' And when they call out his name they're going to scream 'Lebron!' instead of 'LeBron.' It's dirty, but that's how we roll in San Antonio."

"Thank you, Hacksaw."

"Thanks, Hoops. Remember, we're dirty. And if you or anyone you know needs an organ donation while you're in town, give me a call and we'll get you hooked up."

Shut out of my bailout

9/23/2008

"Good morning, sir. Welcome to Bank Till of America. How can I help you?"

"I need some money."

"OK, for what purposes?"

"My family has gotten behind in our bills—no mismanagement, you understand, but just some hard times. You see, my wife just got laid off, two of our three children had unexpected illnesses that weren't fully covered by our health insurance. Gas and food prices are escalating, and it's getting harder for us to make our mortgage payments. We're not extravagant, mind you, but we do need some help."

"So are you asking for a loan, sir?"

"We need a bailout, ma'am."

"I'm sorry, eh, as I look at your information, Mr. Cue—Jonathan Cue, is it?—but based on your resources, we're not able to give you a loan."

"Ma'am, I don't want a loan. I want a bailout."

"I'm sorry, sir, but I don't understand."

"A bailout. I want the same deal you gave to those people in the news, that Fannie Mae woman, that Freddie Mac fellow, the Bear Stearns dude and the Notorious AIG."

"Sir, those are mortgage lending giants, banks and insurance companies, and the bailout given to them was essential to the American economy."

"I understand. And the bailout I want you to give me is essential to my family's economy."

"Sir, without the assistance we give to them, the ramifications would be disastrous for Wall Street and the Fortune 500 companies."

"Ma'am, without the assistance I need you to give me, the ramifications would be disastrous to Main Street, Elm Street and Guadalupe Street, as well as to the unfortunate millions I keep company with."

"I'm sorry, sir. We can't help you."

"But you helped them."

"That's different."

"Why?"

"Because you weren't irresponsible with billions of dollars and they were irresponsible with billions of dollars. Therefore, we must give them billions of dollars more."

"Huh?"

"I know it makes no sense, but that's high finance for you."

"OK, ma'am, I was trying to be reasonable, but since that won't work I'm through asking for a bailout."

"Good."

"Just give me my money, no questions asked."

"Sir?"

"My money. The cash you're using to help Fannie, Freddie and all the other Capitalism Is Great When I'm Making Billions But Socialism Is Greater When I'm Losing Billions folk. That's my money, right?"

"Yes, but—"

"I read where this $700 billion bailout is going to cost every American about $2,300. Is that right?"

"Yes, but—"

"And about $6,000 per household, right?"

"Yes, but—"

"And the national debt costs each American about $30,000 and each taxpayer about $67,000, right?"

"Yes, but—"

"Me and my wife are due $134,000 on the national debt, $6,000 on the bailout. Just give us $140,000 right now and we'll call it even."

"Sir, I'm sorry. That's just not possible."

"So you're not going to do for me what you did for Fannie Mae?"

"No, sir."

"What if my mother's name is Annie Mae?"

"No, sir."

"What if I sing the Bee Gees' 'Fanny Be Tender (With My Love)'?"

"No, sir."

"And you're not going to give me the same deal you gave Freddie Mac?"

"No, sir."

"What if I did a Bernie Mac impersonation? God bless his soul."

"No, sir."

"What if I hummed the theme song from Fred MacMurray's *My Three Sons*?"

"No, sir."

"Well, will you do me one favor?"

"What's that, sir?"

"Next time you use my money for a bailout or to raise the debt, money that I never saw and didn't know I had, could you at least let me hold it for a couple of hours?"

You won't believe—so stay tuned

7/8/2007

YOU WON'T BELIEVE how many consonants are in the sixth paragraph of this column! The answer may surprise and shock you.

I have much love for my brothers and sisters in broadcast news. In fact, YOU WON'T BELIEVE how much love I have for my brothers and sisters in broadcast media. The answer may surprise and shock you.

We're all in the same business, trying to do a little to inform and educate and, depending on your political leanings, taking our cue from Liberal Headquarters in our ongoing quest to undermine America or selling our souls to the corporate and political elite.

But why do newscasts have to repeatedly promote a story by saying, "YOU WON'T BELIEVE," as in, "YOU WON'T BELIEVE where your tax money is going" or "stay tuned because YOU WON'T BELIEVE the latest development in the story"? That's often followed by a prediction of what this unbelievable news will do to you: "It may surprise and shock you." Recently, one of the local weekend anchors, in reporting on an injured criminal suspect, said, "YOU WON'T BELIEVE what he told police about how he got hurt."

I was on my way out the door but OK, I was curious. So I waited to hear what the answer was. Turns out the suspect said that he cut himself jumping a fence.

Now, I can believe that. I've cut myself jumping a fence—I wasn't running from the police—but it wasn't unbelievable that it happened.

I thought the "YOU WON'T BELIEVE" ruse was a local news

tic. But on CNN, Wolf Blitzer, reporting that Democratic presidential candidate John Edwards' wife, Elizabeth, supported gay marriage, intoned, "YOU WON'T BELIEVE where her husband was when he found out." And on MSNBC, Tucker Carlson, talking about a family road trip once taken by Republican presidential candidate Mitt Romney, said, "YOU WON'T BELIEVE what they strapped to the roof of their car."

Now that one did surprise me because the answer was the family dog, and it is hard to believe that a man who wants to be president would put the dog in a box on the car roof for a 12-hour trip.

To all of you talented broadcast journalists who insist on telling me what I won't believe, I have but one thing to say: Don't give me so much credit. Don't overestimate my intelligence. I just might believe it.

I'm gullible and naïve. I still believe in peace and goodwill to all men and women. I still believe that Mrs. Butterworth will talk to me when I put the bottle of pancake syrup on the table. You won't believe how easily I can be taken. You had me at "Hello, welcome to our 10 o'clock newscast."

And I'm not alone. Forty-one percent of the American people still think that Iraq had something to do with 9-11. Many of us are certain that there are strangers in Nigeria who generously want to share their wealth with us. Oh, we'll believe.

Also, it's very possible that what it is you say I won't believe may not be that big of a revelation to begin with. I'm not going to believe that taxpayer money is being wasted? That's neither surprising nor shocking.

Tell me something that I won't believe, like Terrell Owens went through an entire season without causing any controversy, or Gov. Perry is a respected world leader whose counsel is valuable, or a presidential candidate actually said he or she wants to be president because it's satisfying to the ego, has incredible perks and Secret Service protection is just way too cool.

The YOU WON'T BELIEVE routine is used just a little more than that other popular local news promotion of delaying vital news that they say might save lives. Such as, "Someone is stalking your child—we'll tell you who in our 6 o'clock newscast."

No! Tell me now! My child doesn't get home until 6:30. Tell me now and maybe I can save my child before your next newscast.

Or this one: "An everyday household product can kill you in just 4 minutes—we'll have that story for you in 8 minutes."

You won't believe how maddening this can get—or that there were 64 consonants in the sixth paragraph.

Lying their behinds off

1/10/2004

"Hello, everyone. Welcome to *Lying Their Behinds Off*, the nationally syndicated show that puts the spotlight on some of the great liars of today. I'm your host, Fibb Teller.

"Both of today's guests come from the state of Ohio. First, we have Pete Rose, the most prolific hitter in history who accumulated most of those hits with his hometown Cincinnati Reds.

"After 14 years of denying that he bet on baseball games, he finally has admitted that he did indeed gamble on games, including more than 400 on the Reds when he was managing them.

"Next, we have Elecia Battle, the Cleveland woman whose claim to have bought a lottery ticket worth $162 million has been proven false.

"Welcome to both of you. Wow, what are the odds that the week's two big liars would both come from the same state?"

Rose: "About 367,000 to 1, Fibb."

Battle: "Hold on! That's the number I was going to say!"

Teller: "Elecia, while you have apologized, you haven't actually said that you lied. You insist that you did buy a ticket and lost it. In what convenience store did you buy the ticket?"

Battle: "Well, ah, the store, ah, it had a roof and, you know, it had four walls, you know and, oh yeah, it had a door."

Teller: "Pete, for 14 years you have been adamant in your denial that you gambled on baseball. What took you so long to say that you did?"

Rose: "That's not my fault. It's a shame that it took 14 years for a publisher to offer me $1 million to admit that I gambled on baseball."

Teller: "So you're saying that it's only for the money that you're admitting this?"

Rose: "Fibb, for a million bucks I'd admit to being Gypsy Rose Lee. You can bet on that. Ha, I did."

Teller: "You had how many career hits?"

Rose: "4,256."

Battle: "Wait a minute! That's how many hits I had. Honest!"

Teller: "Pete, in your book you write, 'I'm sure I'm supposed to act all sorry or sad or guilty now that I've accepted that I've done something wrong. But you see, I'm just not built that way.' Pete, your lack of remorse has offended many people. Any regrets?"

Rose: "If that has offended people enough to keep me from getting into the Hall of Fame then, OK, I'll say that I'm [he raises his hands to indicate quotation marks] 'sorry' and 'sad' about 'hurting' so many people. If you give me some time, I'll try to come up with some tears to make me really look sincere."

Teller: "Elecia, you have a criminal record that includes assault and credit card fraud. What made you think you could get away with this?"

Battle: "Pure trust. The problem with the world today is that a person's word isn't good enough to be believed—and paid $162 million."

Teller (to Rose, who is punching himself in the face): "Pete, what are you doing?"

Rose: "Trying to hurt myself so I can cry, but I'm just too tough. Can you come back to me in a minute?"

Teller: "Elicia, what have you learned from your experience?"

Battle: "That if I don't admit to lying, I may get a book deal out of this."

Rose: "Fibb! I've got a tear! Hurry, before it goes away!"

Teller: "What made you cry, Pete?"

Rose: "Remembering Sept. 16, 1988, when Tom Browning pitched a perfect game for us and I didn't bet on that game. I'm so sorry."

Clowns—they pop up everywhere

7/19/2008

It's been a couple of weeks since I confessed to a lifelong fear of clowns and rats. God help me if I ever open my front door and see a clown holding a rat.

A few things have happened on the clown front recently. On a Houston freeway, I was with my father, who was driving, when I told him, "Watch out. There's a clown coming up behind you."

"OK," he said.

"No, I really mean it. There's a clown coming up behind you."

A driver dressed as a clown was driving a Volvo. I wasn't too scared because Daddy was packing heat. But it did cross my mind that if there was an accident and the enraged clown attacked us and my father was forced to shoot it, instead of bullets coming out the gun there would be a blue flag with the word "Bang."

And how smart is it to drive as a clown? I've had some experience with DWB, Driving While Black, but isn't there danger of DWC, Driving While Clown?

The greater worry should be if there is an accident. Emergency technicians are among the most professional and dedicated members of any work force. But if you're a paramedic called to a scene and you get there to see an unconscious clown, isn't there the temptation to start cracking up, tears rolling down your cheeks while you're doubled up laughing? You stop, try to put poor Chuckles onto a stretcher but then start laughing again, and you drop him and he bounces off the ground with that boing sound.

Earlier this month, Larry Harmon, who popularized Bozo the Clown, died. I mourned for Mr. Harmon and prayed for his family.

I rejoiced at the death of Bozo and celebrated by blowing clown horns while riding a unicycle through my neighborhood.

I wondered about the deaths of clowns, like how do they get the casket to close over those huge red shoes? I envisioned a clown funeral in which a tiny casket is rolled into the chapel and six clowns, the pallbearers, hop out of it.

But the strangest thing was last week when I was downtown at the Justice Center. I was collecting my things after going through security when a lady approached the security guards to tell them, "There will be someone coming who's a clown dressed as the Grim Reaper. They're here for someone's birthday upstairs so they're all right."

A shiver went down my spine at the words "clown dressed as the Grim Reaper." Those are six words you never imagine being strung together: "clown dressed as the Grim Reaper."

I know, I know. A clown dressed as the Grim Reaper walking the halls of the courthouse. This is too rich. A comic Comstock of silver-plated one-liners. The mother lode of jokes.

But I don't do lawyer jokes, just like I don't do jokes about politicians because they're too easy, too cliché and unnecessarily increase public cynicism. There are a lot of underpaid public servants and even some overpriced attorneys in private practice working hard and doing a lot of good.

"Come on, Cary, cut out the goody-two-shoes smack! This is a big fat pitch hanging over the plate. Be like Josh Hamilton at the home run derby and let her rip. You've got a clown dressed as the Grim Reaper traipsing around the courthouse!"

No, I just can't do it. I'd like to, but it's just not me.

"You pansy! It's a clown! Dressed as the Grim Reaper! Walking around the courthouse where the district attorney, prosecutors, defense attorneys and judges are 'working hard' and doing 'a lot of good.' Metaphors, baby! Metaphors!"

Nope, I won't do it. But when the lady warned the security

guards about the clown dressed as the Grim Reaper, I was hoping to hear one of them ask, "Yes, ma'am, and how is today different from any other day?"

And I felt a pang of sympathy thinking about the first-time offender, waiting to meet his court-appointed attorney, looking up and seeing you-know-who walking into the courtroom.

So there you have it. Last Wednesday afternoon, a clown dressed as the Grim Reaper was at the courthouse. You fill in the blanks.

As for me, next time I'm called for jury duty and want to get out of it, guess what I'm coming dressed as?

"Village" embraces brothers

3/18/2008

It's how you look at it. At first thought, that three brothers have had three mothers and been adopted twice before turning 12 is something sad.

But that's when their lives are seen with eyes focused on what's been lost. With eyes that can appreciate the good things kept and built upon, the story of the Bonsignore brothers is something to be grateful for.

Jeremy and Nathan are 11-year-old twins, and their brother, Desmond, is 10. They were on the front page of this newspaper on Aug. 7, 2000, when *Express-News* reporter Susie Gonzalez profiled them.

The front-page photo showed the boys running on the St. Pius X baseball field with their adoptive mother, Celeste Bonsignore, and her best friend, Kathy Restivo.

The boys began their lives at Providence Home, once the only residential facility in South Texas for HIV babies. Their biological mother was HIV-positive. Babies born to HIV-positive mothers have IIIV antibodies, so they initially test positive. This was the case with the boys, but they soon proved to be free of the deadly disease.

They caught the eye and heart of Bonsignore, a Catholic school principal and teacher who volunteered at Providence Home. When she made the decision to adopt them, it was momentous and challenged conventional wisdom and common sense.

Not only was Bonsignore a single, woman adopting three young boys; she was a 56-year-old single white woman adopting three young black boys. In the summer of 1998, she became not only their mother but also a lifeline to a vibrant and nurturing future.

For her, the oft-quoted African proverb about it taking a village to raise a child wasn't a cliché but a necessity. Back in 2000, she said of her sons, "They are my community babies. They've felt surrounded by love, and they deserve every moment of it. They had a rough start in life, but it's really good for them now."

And because Bonsignore was the principal at St. Piux X School, that parish became their community, their village. Desmond was baptized in the presence of 400 students.

Knowing she also had a responsibility to help her sons understand their African American heritage, Bonsignore filled their home with books, artwork and religious icons that helped teach and celebrate that heritage.

Bonsignore's time as a mother was the best and most rewarding of her life, and she decided to retire after the school year ended in the spring of 2006 so she could spend more time with the boys. On Oct. 26 of that year, the day after her 64th birthday, she was diagnosed with a brain tumor. Less than three weeks later, on Nov. 14, she died.

The community embraced its babies; there was never any doubt about it. In her will, Bonsignore named her best friend, Restivo, as the boys' guardian.

When Restivo, a teacher at Little Flower Catholic School, talked about adopting them, they were excited and wouldn't have it any other way, although Nathan said wistfully, "We're going to have three mothers."

For children to get to a third mother means they've experienced considerable heartbreak. But for children to get to a third mother also translates into being wanted and loved. The Bonsignore brothers have never been separated, never spent a night in a children's shelter or foster home.

Last Friday, when the boys and Restivo walked down the

second-floor hall of the old courthouse, they were cheered by two dozen well-wishers, family and friends who have been cheering for them for 10 years. The boys fidgeted with their ties and smiled.

Judge Peter Sakai, who in 1998 finalized the brothers' adoption to Bonsignore, was now finalizing their adoption to Restivo. When he called them to stand before him at the bench, he invited everyone in attendance to stand with them.

"This is what we call a no-return policy," Sakai quipped.

After papers were signed and pictures taken, Restivo and her sons walked out of the courthouse. Nathan now has one word to describe having three mothers: "Cool."

On Friday afternoon, Jeremy, Nathan and Desmond Bonsignore walked on a downtown street. Heading for a celebratory lunch of Mexican food, they were surrounded by their mother, Kathy Restivo, and some of their family and friends.

It was just the way Celeste Bonsignore had planned it. Their community had their backs.

Even simple lessons can be lost on well-meaning children

5/2/2001

This is a strange story. But not one without its lessons.

Early Saturday morning, Brenda Rodriguez's 9-year-old son Jorge left their apartment in Cassiano Homes along with some friends. They were members of Brewer Elementary's school band and were going to perform in the King William parade.

At the corner of Loma Vista and Hamilton, two well-dressed men in a green pickup stopped and asked the kids if anyone wanted to make $10 by going with them to get a dead cat from under a house.

None of the children knew the man, but Jorge took them up on the offer, got into the truck and drove off.

His friends ran to tell Mrs. Rodriguez, who immediately called 911.

Jorge says the men drove to a white house off San Pedro near North Star Mall. Along with the men, he went under the house and smelled and saw the dead cat but didn't retrieve it. He may have become scared, but exactly why he didn't get the cat isn't clear.

At some point, he told the men that he wanted to go home. They told him they would quickly take him back.

The three got back into the truck and, Jorge says, drove to another house where the men went inside to change clothes. Jorge stayed in the truck, but by now he was scared enough to see if he could start the truck by himself and leave.

The men came back outside and drove him back to Cassiano Homes. Jorge says one of the men, apparently upset that he didn't get the cat, began insulting him.

"He started using bad words," the boy says.

When they got to Cassiano Homes, they were met by policemen and Jorge's worried family and neighbors. The two men were arrested and taken away.

Mrs. Rodriguez says she was told by an officer that the men were arrested on priors and that she couldn't press charges of kidnapping because what happened to her son was a "business deal" between him and the men.

As of Tuesday afternoon, the police report hadn't been completed, so many things remain unclear.

Mrs. Rodriguez claims the two men have been released from jail and that their truck has been spotted at least twice in the neighborhood, including yesterday when she saw it.

"I'm worried about my son," she says. "What if they come back for him again?"

Jorge says the men didn't touch or harm him.

"Are you telling the truth?" his mother asks.

He nods his head.

She still can't believe that her son would get into a stranger's vehicle. "My husband and I are very shocked," she says. "We've told him time and time again about this. But he has a noble heart and always wants to help people. This makes you think if you're doing the right thing."

Gilbert De La Portilla, a crime prevention specialist for the SAPD, says that even kids who know better will make mistakes.

"You can tell them something, but they can do the very opposite," he notes. "But they have to be taught that a stranger is someone you don't know."

Postscript: As I was leaving the Rodriguez's home, Jorge, who'd known me for less than an hour, asked, "Do you think you can drop me off at the Good Samaritan Center?"

I politely declined.

Target just couldn't have any more rude bell-ringers

Somewhere in the home of a top executive at Target.

"You did what?"

"I fired the Salvation Army's bell ringers."

"The people with the bells and red kettles who are always out in front of your stores during the Christmas season raising money for the needy?"

"Yes, that's them."

"Well, you must have had a good reason, dear. I'm sure it had nothing to do with all that talk of a nationwide trend of retailers prohibiting all soliciting on their property. They must have really done something horrible to force you to make that painful decision."

"Uh—"

"Well, what did they do? I'm sure there must have been some awful complaints made against them by customers."

"Ah, yes, there were. Awful complaints, just awful."

"Like what?"

"Well, ah, they would look at people."

"Look at people?"

"Yeah, they would look at people and, ah, not say anything to them and, ah, then they would just smile."

"Not say anything? You mean they wouldn't say anything to people other than ask them to make a donation?"

"See, actually, they never technically asked people to make donations."

"What do you mean by 'technically'?"

"Well, they never opened their mouths and made the sounds

and used the words to actually ask people to make donations, but in their minds they were hoping they would."

"Children, it's time for dinner! So when people didn't put money in the kettles, the bell ringers would insult them?"

"Uh, no, they wouldn't say anything to them. They'd just smile but, oh, it would be a creepy smile. And sometimes they'd even tell them to have a good day, but what they were really saying was, 'If you can't give any money to the needy, get out of my face.'"

"Did they threaten to assault them with the bells for not giving any money?"

"No."

"Were they rude to people who put money in the kettle?"

"Yes! That's it. They were incredibly rude to the people who put money in the kettles. Yeah. That's why we had to kick them off our premises."

"No children, Daddy isn't going to fire Santa Claus. Dear, that's awful and inconsiderate on the part of the bell ringers. What rude things did they say to the generous customers who put money in the kettles?"

"They would say 'Thank you.'"

"Thank you? That's not rude."

"Oh, but it was the tone in their voice and the way they said 'you.' It was very sinister. And sometimes they'd say 'Merry Christmas,' but if you listened carefully they were really telling you 'I've got your money now so get out of my face.' And their smiles, those creepy, friendly smiles."

"Children, stop crying. I promise you that Daddy isn't going to take Rudolph the Red-Nosed Reindeer to the pound to be put to sleep. Well, dear, I'm sure you did the right thing. Only ding-a-lings would force people to think about the less fortunate at Christmas."

If gravy's on ballot,
will you vote then?

3/14/2006

A week ago today in Texas was Election Day, one of the signature days of a democracy. A day when citizens, concerned about the issues that affect their lives and the people who will work on those issues, march to the polls to make their voice heard.

It's a day when politicians, eager to prove that they should be the Chosen One, send out the clarion call summoning the free and the brave to cast the votes that generations fought and died for. A day when voters answer that call and say, "Yes, I'm a citizen of a democracy and I'll proudly exercise my right to vote."

The citizenry of this great state woke up last Tuesday morning, saw what day it was, knew what the responsibility was, heard the clarion call of the politicians and, in a resounding, near-unanimous voice, yawned and asked, "How many more hours until *American Idol* comes on?"

Last week, less than 10 percent of registered voters in Texas voted in the primary election. In Bexar County, only 7 percent of registered voters cast ballots.

7 percent turned out to vote.

You can buy milk that has 2 percent fat, which means that fat has almost as high a turnout in a gallon of milk as Bexar County voters did in last week's election.

7 percent?

It wasn't so long ago that voting was so important to South Texans that they'd vote twice in an election and wouldn't let anything, including death, keep them from going to the polls.

It's as if people think that it's a themocracy we live in and that it's "them"—everybody else—who are supposed to decide how their government is run.

Up until November, there will be much discussion about how to counter voter apathy and increase turnout in the general election. Voting is so low in most U.S. elections that a turnout of one-third of registered voters would be welcome.

Such discussions of increasing voter turnout should stop now. In Texas, and especially Bexar County, we have a chance to do something extraordinary, historic and more attainable. A 7 percent voter turnout is closer to 0 percent than it is to 33 percent voter turnout.

We've dropped this low, so why not drop more, until we become the first major county to have 0 percent voter turnout for an election? If you're going to be bad, don't just be ordinarily bad. Be the all-time baddest.

Any county in any election can have an abysmally low turnout. But it takes a truly apathetic county of "I just don't give a damn" proportions to have no one care enough to vote.

Some will say this is ridiculous. I look at last Tuesday's results and say, yeah, but it's possible.

If this idea doesn't catch hold, then at least we should have something that inspires people and stokes their passions—like gravy. When it was reported that gravy would not be served at this year's Cowboy Breakfast, the community rose up in loud and indignant protest and demanded their free gravy.

Organizers heard them, feared their wrath, reversed their decision and served gravy. Such a creamy and delectable example of people power and democracy in action.

So I say let 'em eat gravy. Beginning with next month's runoff, Bexar County election officials should give every registered voter who takes the time to vote a free pint of cream gravy.

It will then be left to the campaigns of those running for office to do a better job of providing some meat.

Give her credit
for a worldwide movement

....

"You may do that."

With those words, spoken to the bus driver who threatened to have her arrested for refusing to surrender her seat to a white man, Rosa Parks ignited one of history's greatest revolutions.

"You may do that."

The civility and dignified defiance of these words and the refusal to move by this lady of impeccable character and manners would set the tone for the nonviolent drama that would be played out before an enthralled and impressionable world.

"You may do that."

Arlam Carr Jr., whose 94-year-old mother, Johnnie, grew up with Parks, says, "She was very humble and quiet. But she was tired of injustice and said she wasn't getting up."

In December 1955, Thelma Glass was a professor of geography and history at Alabama State University and a member of the Women's Political Council. She was one of the women who distributed the first leaflets calling for a boycott of the city buses.

"She was a perfect lady," the 89-year-old Glass says of Parks. "She was very compassionate and very serious about doing the right thing and helping people. When I met her she was working with young people in the NAACP."

I've been in Montgomery since Saturday night on a reporting trip on the upcoming 50th anniversary of the bus boycott that launched the modern civil rights movement.

Since being here, I've had the strangest feeling that Mrs. Parks would die while I was in Montgomery. It was heightened Monday morning while I visited the Rosa Parks Library and Museum, built at Montgomery Street and Molton at the site of her arrest.

A little after 10 on Monday night, after learning that Mrs. Parks had died in Detroit at the age of 92, I drove the short distance from my hotel to where her legend was cast.

I stopped for a minute before continuing down Montgomery Street where it curves into expansive Dexter Avenue. Up ahead, just a few blocks away, the state Capitol was illuminated, with the American and Alabama flags flapping atop it in the cold night air. Across the street from the Capitol was Dexter Avenue King Memorial Church, the brick church from which Martin Luther King Jr. led the boycott.

For 20 minutes I drove up and down Montgomery and Dexter, marveling that these few blocks, now empty and ghostly quiet, had been filled with a majestic history that transformed this country. All because of a woman saying "You may do that."

On Tuesday, black bows were on the front doors of the Rosa Parks Library and Museum and large red ribbons, like roses, decorated the fountain at Court Square. Throughout downtown Montgomery, including on top of the Capitol, the U.S. and Alabama flags flew at half-staff.

"People like Rosa Parks, their legacy lives on forever," says Glass. "She was the person who was needed at that time."

She's called the Mother of the Civil Rights Movement. But given the influence the movement has had on subsequent movements for liberation and justice around the world, couldn't Rosa Parks also be called the Mother of the International Human Rights Movement?

You may do that.

A politician who needs to shut up, not 'fess up

3/27/2008

Somebody, anybody, everybody please perform a public service that will bring each of us great relief. Somebody, anybody, everybody, please stop New York Gov. David Paterson before he confesses again.

On St. Patrick's Day, Paterson's job title was elevated, to great and popular acclaim, from lieutenant governor to governor when he took the oath of office, succeeding the disgraced, self-righteous and hypocritical Eliot Spitzer.

Hours later, Paterson confessed to being unfaithful to his wife in the past. Then he and she confessed that she had been unfaithful to him. Then he confessed that he'd had affairs with not just one but several women.

Then he confessed that when he and his wife reconciled they went to the same Days Inn room in which he'd had some of his trysts. By then the TMI (Too Much Information) Train had gone off the tracks. But Paterson, still chugging along, this week confessed to using marijuana and cocaine when he was in his early 20s.

Props to the governor for wanting to get in front of any bad news and get it out of the way so he can concentrate on governing. But short of some wicked and illegal deeds, is it necessary for us to know each and every misstep of a politician and—

"Hey, Clack."

Oh, hello, Gov. Paterson. I was just writing about you.

"I know. Listen, I wanted to confess that I stole your college girlfriend away from you. Just thought you should know that."

OK, Governor, that no longer concerns me, but thanks for

being upfront about it. Now, where was I? Oh yeah, is it really necessary for us to know about each misstep made by politicians? They're human and as flawed as—

"Clack, it's Paterson again. A few years ago I borrowed a friend's car without telling him and I wrecked it. To this day he thinks someone else stole it but, hey, I confess to doing it."

But Governor, you're legally blind.

"That's why I wrecked it. I just wanted to put that out there."

OK, now let me continue. Politicians are as fallible as the rest of us and shouldn't be expected to have flawless personal histories. Still, Paterson's candor is a bit refreshing and . . . What is it now, Governor?

"I want to confess that in 1998 I robbed a bank in Manhattan and got away with more than $3 million."

Thanks, Governor, but—

"Did I confess to my hemorrhoid problem?"

Governor, please! Let me continue. While we don't want our elected officials to be stunning hypocrites in the mold of Spitzer, neither should we be hypocrites and hold them to standards we ourselves don't always . . . Governor, what is it?

"I shot a man in Reno, just to watch him die."

That's a line from "Folsom Prison Blues" by Johnny Cash!

"It is?"

Yes.

"All right. I confess to helping Johnny Cash shoot a man in Reno just to watch him die."

Governor, this column isn't the place for you to be baring your soul and making all of these confessions.

"You're right. I'll go to that Catholic Church I passed on the way over here."

Good. Now, in conclusion, perhaps we expect too much from our public officials and should . . . Yes, Governor?

"The grassy knoll, Dallas, November of 1963, I con—"

This mutt doesn't exactly inspire brotherly feelings

1/1/2003

On the night after Christmas, in my grandmother's living room, I almost killed my new brother.

This was after he annoyed me, showing off by spinning on his hind legs while our father fed him.

I don't like my new brother, the one they call Big Shot. The one who's a dog.

Somewhere in his life, my father, a man of some accomplishment, lost it and began referring to his chocolate-colored Doberman, Rambo, and his white poodle, Shadow, as his children.

As I've mentioned before, this hit me a few years ago when he called out, "Son!"

"Yeah?" I answered.

"I wasn't talking to you. I was talking to Rambo."

In their Houston home, my father and stepmother have more studio photographs of Rambo and Shadow than pictures of children and grandchildren. The dogs are better dressed and groomed.

Therapy, medication and yoga have allowed me to finally accept the two as my siblings. To keep up with them and win my father's approval, I've learned how to sit up and roll over, and I can fetch a ball like no other man or animal.

But along comes Big Shot, an ill-tempered, loud-mouthed, arrogant, selfish, biting and petulant white Maltese that was found recently in the street near my father's house. (OK, except for the white Maltese part he sounds a lot like me.)

A $900 Maltese doesn't just show up without anyone trying to find it. Unless the owners realize it's the devil's dog and want to unload it on some nice people who treat dogs as children, buy them caps and gowns for studio photos at obedience school graduation day, and spend thousands of dollars a year on them.

Hey, what about the guy who thinks the Doberman and poodle are his sons?

Over the Christmas holiday, Big Shot made his first visit to our grandmother's house in San Antonio—sadly, my grandmother has come to look upon these dogs as her grandsons—and it's where he almost died at my hand.

When the Maltese from Hell wasn't barking like a canine on crack, he showed off. As he did his little trick on hind legs while my father fed him a piece of meat, my sister asked me, "Is that how Dad fed you when you were little?"

"Of course. That's how I developed my calf muscles."

My feelings about Big Shot, who isn't even liked by Rambo and Shadow, spilled out when he bothered Rambo to the point of making the Doberman bark and chase him through the house.

"Kill him, Rambo!" I shouted.

Later, Big Shot stole one of my grandmother's slippers. Having already guessed that my share of my father's inheritance is going to the dogs, I thought that by rescuing my grandmother's shoe I still had a chance at her inheritance.

I chased Big Shot, who jumped into my father's lap. I shouted at the dog as I tried to pull the slipper from its mouth.

"Listen, you SOB," (and I'm confident of the accuracy of my characterization), "give me that shoe before I knock your head off!"

Everyone in the house stopped and stared at me as my fist was cocked to hit a little dog with whom I was having a tug-of-war over a pink slipper.

"Ah, something came over me," I tried to explain. "Must have been the fruitcake."

Big Shot, your day will come. Everyone else, have a happy new year.

The speech a segregationist, and dad, should have made

12/27/2003

Columnist's note: The family of Strom Thurmond has acknowledged that Essie Mae Washington-Williams, whose mother was black, is the late senator's daughter. In the summer of 1964, Thurmond was considering switching political parties. Here is the news conference he should have held back then.

"To the press and to the good people of South Carolina watching on television and listening over the radio, I thank you for giving me a few minutes of your time.

"I know that all of you are expecting me to announce whether I am switching over to the Republican Party from the Democratic Party. But today, I'd like to discuss something of greater importance than politics and ideology. Instead, I want to talk about truth, family and redemption.

"Throughout my political career in which you have blessed me with the opportunity to serve you as governor, United States senator and a run for the White House, there have been rumors that I once fathered a black child.

"Today, I acknowledge that I am indeed the father of a black woman named Essie Mae Washington-Williams, who I will now ask to step forward and be at my side for the remainder of this news conference.

"It has been difficult for me to come to this place on this day to admit this. I can't say what compels me to make this confession, except that it is the right thing to do and I can no longer, in good conscience, deny my child the public acknowledgment of the paternity she deserves.

"Here in 1964, there may be no bigger hypocrite in the United States than me. A politician who has based his political career on segregation and arguing against the mixing of races when I fathered a child by a black woman. A politician who advocated for laws that would deny my daughter and her mother voting rights and all of the other rights guaranteed to them by our Constitution.

"I am not alone in this. For generations throughout the South, black children have been fathered by white men like myself. Men whose words said one thing during the day but whose actions said quite another at night.

"In my defense, and it's meager, I have provided financial support for Essie Mae, visited her when she was a student at South Carolina State and welcomed her into the governor's mansion, albeit the back door entrance, and into my Senate chambers.

"I have never denied a relationship with her, but I have never been forthright about the biological nature of our relationship.

"To Essie Mae and to her mother, Carrie Butler, may she rest in peace, I apologize for not being a better man.

"I have said and done things that have hurt many people. To everyone I've hurt, I apologize and pledge to do better. Old habits and attitudes die hard, but if they are hurtful they must die. I have met with Dr. Martin Luther King and look forward to more meetings with him as to how I can help reverse the segregationist tide of our history.

"Today's announcement may effectively end my political career, but I can no longer deny history or my child. Nor can I continue to deny her and others like her the rights given to them by God.

"If you want to call me a segregationist, do so. If you want to call me a hypocrite, do so.

"But from this day forward, be sure that you also call me Essie Mae Washington-Williams' father."

Angel affirms a girl's faith

10/22/2006

This is a little story about a little girl who lost her dog and found an angel.

Until this summer, Greg and Joy Scrivener's family included three children and a 14-year-old black and white mutt named Abbey who was older than the combined ages of their children.

In mid-August, Abbey died, upsetting the family, especially 4-year-old Meredith. The day after Abbey's death, a tearful Meredith, holding a piece of paper, told her mother that she wanted to write a letter to God. Joy proceeded to write down what her daughter told her. The letter read:

Dear God,

Will you please take care of our dog, Abbey? She died yesterday and she is in heaven now. We hope that Abbey is OK now and that she isn't sick anymore. We love you for letting us have Abbey even though she died. We are sending pictures of Abbey in the little envelopes so that you can see what she looks like and you will know her when you see her.

Love, Meredith Claire

PS: Mommy wrote it after Mer told her the words.

The letter with pictures was addressed "To: God in Heaven" and had the family's return address on it. Mother and daughter walked to the Brook Hollow post office, and Meredith dropped her letter into the mailbox.

For the next two weeks, Meredith cried whenever she thought about Abbey, which was often.

When the Scriveners returned from a Labor Day trip, they found a package wrapped in gold on their front porch that was addressed "To: Mer." Inside the package was a book by Fred Rogers (of *Mr. Rogers' Neighborhood*) titled *When a Pet Dies*.

The letter Meredith had sent to God was in its opened envelope and taped to the book's front cover. On the back cover was a handwritten note on pink paper that read:

Dear Mer,

I know that you will be happy to find out that Abbey arrived safely and soundly in heaven. Having the picture you sent to me was a big help! I recognized Abbey right away!

You know, Mer, she isn't sick anymore. Her spirit is here with me, just like it stays in your heart—young and running and playing. Abbey loved being your dog, you know. Since we don't need our bodies in heaven, I don't have any pockets! So, I am sending you your beautiful letter back with the pictures—so that you will have this little memory book to keep.

One of my angels is taking care of this for me. I hope this book will help. Thank you for your beautiful letter. Thank your mother for sending it. What a wonderful mother you have; I picked her just for you.

Signed,
God, and one of his special angels who wrote this letter after God told her the words

Joy Scrivener says that the letter and gift have comforted Meredith but didn't surprise her. "She wasn't surprised because she had such faith that her letter was going to get to God." She says that her oldest child, 6-year-old Andy, who reads the book to Meredith, is impressed.

"He thought it was pretty special his sister got a book from the angel."

Joy thought about making inquiries at the post office to find out who sent the package but decided against it.

"I kind of like not knowing," she says. "I don't know who took the time to do it, but it was an angel. We all think about doing these things, but no one takes the time to do it."

Jury duty: Bonding, respect, $6 a day

8/19/2007

It used to be when I received a jury summons, I cringed and tried to schedule a lobotomy for the same day of my appearance. When doctors informed me that I'd already maxed out on the number of lobotomies I could have, I looked for other ways to avoid jury duty.

Wearing my Black Panther outfit and yelling "Free Huey Newton!" in front of the courthouse was promising until someone told me that Huey Newton had been dead for several years.

"Oh," I replied. "Well, I guess the brother's free now."

Then there was walking into the jury room and announcing "Party at the DA's office for everyone acquitted today."

But through the years my thinking changed, and I thought it wouldn't be such a bad thing to serve on a jury. Nothing else would make people stand up out of respect when I walked into a room. And, hey, $6 a day is $6 a day.

So recently, I sat in the Central Jury Room with a few hundred of my fellow citizens. Just writing that makes me feel proud: "fellow citizens." As I looked around, my heart spilled over with nationalistic pride as I reflected on how uniquely American this experience was.

Several hundred registered voters in a great democracy answering their government's call to serve on a body to determine the guilt or innocence of another human being; called to listen and sift through the facts so that justice will be rendered; called into service because each of us has the right to a jury trial—and each and every one of us hoping that somebody else would be picked to be on a jury and that we would get to go home early.

Amelia (Mellie) Cardona is the longtime central jury bailiff.

She has a wonderful and riveting voice. Her buildup to her intro-
duction of Judge Peter Sakai was so dramatic that I anticipated
her saying, "AND NOW! PUT YOUR HANDS TOGETHER
FOR THE MINISTER OF JUSTICE, THE BABE RUTH OF
BARRISTERS. LET'S HEAR IT FOR THE HONORABLE
JUDGE PETER SAKAI!"

There was a moment of confusion when we all stood up, took
our oath and said, "I do."

"What just happened?" someone asked.

"I don't know," I answered. "But I think either we all just got
married or we're being shipped to Iraq."

Sadness ensued when they called out the names of a few dozen
people who were being allowed to go home. As they were exiting, I
told them, "Wait! You can't just leave like this. We had a moment.
I think it was doing the oath, but we bonded."

One of the great things about being called for jury duty is that
they give you a white badge to wear that says "Bexar Juror." It
lifts your self-esteem and fills you with an overwhelming sense of
power, righteousness and unbending authority. I walked through
the hallways dispensing judgments of guilty or innocent.

When I went to lunch with a friend who's a judge, I strutted
down the street knowing that we were the judge and jury.

Around 2 o'clock, I was ready to go home. It was becoming
clear they weren't going to select me for a jury (afraid of the
Clack brand of justice, I presume), and they were just messing
with me.

When the clerks walk to the microphone in front of the jury
room to name the people who can leave, everyone leans forward
in anticipation. When their names aren't called they sigh and fall
back in their seats. When they hear their names it's as if they've
just been called by *The Price Is Right* to *come on down*.

At one point, one of the clerks announced, "In 45 minutes we
can begin releasing you."

Release? Are we hostages?

When she came back she said, "At this point I'm going to release another group of you."

When I didn't hear my name called, I started to write a letter to be smuggled out to my family telling them that if I didn't make it out alive to dispose of the black box in the master bedroom closet of my house.

But someone told me that my name was called.

"I didn't hear it," I said.

"They said Gary."

"You're kidding." (Some things you can't make up.)

Sure enough, Gary and Cary were released.

I look forward to my next jury summons. For some people, it's their civic duty. For me, it's my Sunday column and $6.

Valerie presses on through pain

3/12/2006

Columnist's note: I've written about this child for so long that she's no longer a child, and I've gained a lot more gray hair. In the early morning hours of April 20, 1994, 8-year-old Valerie Casias was sleeping in her grandmother's house when drive-by shooters opened fire, hitting her four times. Her spine was shattered, and she was paralyzed from the waist down. On the one-year anniversary of the shooting, I wrote a front-page story on her, and I have written about her each year since then, except last year.

The last step she took, perhaps the last one she'll ever take, was lifting her foot off of the floor to lie down to sleep on her grandmother's living room couch. But she keeps moving on even though there have been times when moving forward with her life seemed impossible and not worth the effort and constant pain.

Valerie Casias is now 20 years old. She has blossomed from a cute little girl in a wheelchair into a beautiful young woman in a wheelchair, and she still sometimes finds it hard to believe more than half of her life has been spent in that chair.

She graduated from John Jay High School two years ago and since last August has lived alone in an apartment, something that her family didn't want but that she felt she had to do.

"I was scared at first," she says. "But I'm proud for doing it on my own and not having to count on anyone."

Valerie still wants to be a pediatrician but has had to postpone college until she undergoes surgery to repair the broken rod that was there to keep her spine straight. The operation, which will be her 16th, can't happen until her doctor refers her to a surgeon. But that hasn't happened yet.

Of the five young men responsible for her shooting, only

one remains in prison. Last fall she received a letter from the Department of Criminal Justice informing her that he was up for parole. She asked if she could write him a letter.

The letter, which she is still writing, begins, "My name is Valerie and I'm the reason you're in jail right now."

She goes on to say that the last thing she wants is for him to feel sorry for her but that she just wanted him to understand what her life has been like for the last 12 years, a life she describes as revolving around doctors' appointments, surgeries and constant pain. She writes that she still finds it difficult to accept that she'll never walk again.

As I read her letter, I'm shocked to learn that, while in high school, she attempted suicide.

"Pills," she says when I ask her about it.

Ever since she was a little girl, Valerie has wanted to meet her assailants. She's not bitter or vengeful toward them, something her grandmother, Alicia Garcia, who has just stopped by the apartment, admires but can't understand.

"I'd be resentful," she says.

Only recently, when Valerie read her letter to her, did Garcia learn of the suicide attempt.

She shakes her head at the thought and, in that way only grandmothers can, admonishes Valerie about considering something so selfish and hurtful to those who love her. Theirs is an enormously affectionate relationship filled with laughter and bickering.

"We're like a couple," says Garcia.

"I'm hardheaded," says Valerie.

"Nobody else knows the pain she goes through day in and day out," says Garcia. "She tries to hide the pain, but I know better. Sometimes there are setbacks, but she starts pushing again and wants to go through with whatever it is she wants to do. She wants to be a pediatrician. Children love her and she loves children. I pray that God is with her and gives her the courage. She *can* be a doctor."

Valerie has always had a remarkably calm and unflappable demeanor.

"It takes a lot to get me mad and frustrated. But sometimes I break dishes to relieve stress." She smiles. "So basically, all my dishes are broken. One time I was breaking dishes and my little brother was getting scared so I gave him one and said, 'Here, you want to break one?'"

She bakes but can't cook.

"I'm probably the only person who can burn eggs."

She likes her apartment complex but doesn't go outside much, except when she's leaving, because "Guys try to hit on me."

She sees herself one day having her own family.

"First I have to find myself a boyfriend."

She spends time with friends, some of whom she will travel with to Seattle this week on her first airplane ride.

Asked if she still gets the feeling that she wants to give up, Valerie answers in a soft voice, "Sometimes."

"I hope you don't ever do that again, mama," her grandmother says. "After all we've been through."

In a voice that's stronger and more certain, Valerie says, "I'm not going to let myself give up anymore."

Oh, baby, chest isn't best place

5/16/2006

If the driver of the silver car, who may have caught me eyeing his wife or girlfriend while we both waited at a red light at S. W. Military and Zarzamora on Saturday afternoon, is reading this, man, I apologize.

No disrespect was intended. Your car was to the left of mine, and as we waited for the green light I did find myself staring at your lady, which broaches the protocol of not staring at another guy's lady when he's with her.

Even worse, I was staring at her chest, which no gentleman under any circumstance is supposed to do, unless, of course, the gentleman and the lady are in a situation where to not stare at her chest would be an insult.

Again, no disrespect intended and I apologize if any offense was taken. It's just that I couldn't help but notice her chest and couldn't avert my eyes from the lovely bulge of that chest. So, yes, I stared in amazement and wonder at that lovely bulge, amazed that it was a baby she held to her chest and wondering what the Hades were y'all not thinking about?

Both you and your lady looked as if you were in your 20s so you're young, this may be your first baby and you may not know all that you should about caring for babies or the laws of physics and what can happen to a baby being held by its mother in a moving vehicle when the vehicle is suddenly no longer moving.

Your lady didn't appear to be of more than average size, but the force of her body against the dashboard with your baby in between would have made her first Mother's Day an unforgettable one.

Still, I'd hoped that somewhere between conceiving your baby, welcoming your baby into the world and putting your baby in your car you'd have thought that it might be a good idea to strap your baby in a car seat.

I couldn't tell if you and your lady had your seat belts on and kind of hope you didn't. Not that I'd wish anything bad for the two of you, but it might be better to think buckling up is something that never crosses your mind than to know you took the precaution to protect yourselves but not your baby.

By happy—or not so happy—coincidence, the National Highway Traffic Safety Administration has just issued a report that says 48 million people don't regularly wear seat belts.

One can make a libertarian argument that if adults don't want to wear seat belts and want to increase their risk of being killed by not doing so, that's their right, unless their accidents drive up the insurance costs of drivers who do wear seat belts.

No such argument exists for children, for whom mandatory restraint is necessary if they're going to have the chance to live long enough to be able to make the libertarian case for themselves as adults.

Businesses place messages on their trucks asking how well the driver is driving and a phone number to report bad driving.

Perhaps there ought to be bumper stickers that, at the very least, instruct other drivers to honk their horns at vehicles in which children are unrestrained, standing in the bed of a pickup, sitting on the lap of an adult in the front seat or being held in someone's arms.

Maybe that would do a little to reduce the number of children tattooing windshields in crashes or being turned into tiny human projectiles launched on streets and highways.

So, again, to the driver of the silver car, I didn't mean to stare at your lady's chest. It's just that your lady's chest isn't where your baby should be while you're driving.

Saying goodbye to my Afro
is a hairy proposition

5/12/2001

Dear 'fro,

I see you coming back into other guys' lives, and now you want to get your follicles in me.

I can't let that happen. I can't let you mess with my head. I'm used to living without you.

Baby, I can't lie. I'm tempted by your charms and the memories I have of you. I think about you often. How can I not when each time I look in the mirror I see a shadow of you? Yeah, baby, I admit it, we were good together.

I think back to when we first hooked up. Before you, I had nothing, just a patch of hair on top and not much on the side. Your standard chili bowl haircut.

Then you came into my life when I was 12 and covered my head with your warm and woolly love. 'Fro, you were such a cute little thing back then. As you grew, I grew to love you more.

You got big, but not too big. Going by Jackson 5 Afro standards, you weren't as huge as Michael or Jermaine.

You were more of a Tito and Marlon.

You were big enough for my baseball cap to fly off when I ran, and when the baseball cap came off, I had ring around the 'fro.

Not only did you look good, but you could do some cool things. I could put pens, folded dollar bills, even coins in you and forget about them until the next day.

One time my brother was missing and we didn't find him until I combed you the next morning, and out he fell.

We had our rough moments, love. Life with you was no easy comb-through.

Sometimes I couldn't get the Afro comb or the red, green and black Afro pick through your kinks. My steel rake, the "cake cutter," which doubled as a not-so-concealed weapon sticking out of my right hip pocket, had to dig in deep to unknot you.

Sometimes I'd hurt my scalp with the "cake cutter," trying to untangle you, but that didn't bother me because I'd do anything for you.

I pampered you, my love. I'd get you braided to keep you light and loose. I gave you the best Afro sheen to make the combing easier and coated you with the best hair spray that my mama bought at the Afro store in Alamo Plaza. I remember that coconut was your favorite.

Like Marvin Gaye, I did it just to keep you satisfied.

I wasn't perfect. I didn't always get all of the grooves out of you but, baby, I never abused and dishonored you by leaving you for a Geri-curl.

Yes, our time together was good. Then I strayed. A barber came between us, accidentally cutting off more hair than I wanted.

It upset me until I was soothed by the feel of the wind skating against my scalp. I liked that feeling, 'fro. I realized my scalp needed time to breathe. And, frankly, the new look was low-maintenance.

So it was goodbye.

Now you're back, wanting to grow on me again. Even trying to make me jealous.

Don't think I haven't been noticing what you're doing. Seducing the young high school and middle school kids the way you seduced me. Latching on to young studs like Kobe Bryant and the singer Maxwell.

It won't work, 'fro. To them, it's just a fad. It was more meaningful for us.

It was a matter of cultural pride. I wore you like James Brown singing, "Say it loud! I'm black and I'm proud."

With me, you stood up and said, "Look at me. I'm nappy and free!"

I still love you, 'fro. But not like I used to. If I took you back now, I'd only use you to grow long enough to turn into braids. You deserve better.

Let's just kiss and say goodbye, my love. We'll always have the '70s.

Mind was Malcolm X's power

5/17/2000

When he crashed to the stage of the Audubon Ballroom in Harlem, his body riddled by gunshots fired by black men he sought to save, Malcolm X was the most feared and misunderstood black man in America.

He was feared because, unlike any other black leader before him, he spoke with an electric and searing candor about the brutality of racism and the consequences if it didn't end, yet he did not release blacks from their responsibility to be empowered and self-sufficient.

He was misunderstood because few realized the evolution he was undergoing. At the time, most of the nation and media treated his murder as that of a minor demagogue who got what he deserved.

Thirty-five years after his death, Malcolm, who would have turned 75 Friday, is better understood and appreciated, recognized as the supremely gifted, honest and inspiring leader he was.

To dismiss him as a violent black racist is to reveal an ignorance about the interesting contours of his short life.

He has emerged as an international icon, the subject of a Spike Lee movie, *Malcolm X*, that garnered Denzel Washington an Academy Award nomination. His voice is heard on the most politically conscious of rap songs. His posthumous life story, *The Autobiography of Malcolm X*, is one of the 20th century's great autobiographies. *Time* magazine named it one of the top 10 nonfiction books of the century.

Indeed, the life story told in that book makes Malcolm the singular figure he was. Of the major figures assassinated in the

United States during the 1960s, Malcolm came the furthest to a position of leadership. Few public figures have exhibited such an amazing capacity for growth.

There were actually three Malcolms. There was Malcolm Little, a thieving, pimping, drug-dealing thug whose seven years in prison were the most important of his life.

There was Malcolm X, who became the fiery voice and face of the Black Muslims and lashed out at "white devils" as he articulated the anger of black America.

Then there was El-Hajj Malik El-Shabazz, the name he took after he broke with Elijah Muhammad and the Nation of Islam, made his pilgrimage to Mecca and embraced true Islam.

This was the Malcolm who, for the first time in his life, recognized the oneness of humanity, the Malcolm who, in a letter from Mecca, wrote, "I have never before seen sincere and true brotherhood practiced by all colors together, irrespective of their color. . . . But on this pilgrimage, what I have seen, and experienced, has forced me to rearrange much of my thought-patterns previously held, and to toss aside some of my previous conclusions."

Malcolm possessed many qualities that would have made him a memorable figure: a devotion to the oppressed, a sharp intellect, a mesmerizing oratory and a devastating ability as a debater.

But if one lesson should be learned from his life, it is that people can be redeemed and transformed into heroes.

Malcolm did this through the power of the spirit and knowledge. While he was imprisoned, books, along with Islam, made him the person he became. He attacked his ignorance by reading up to 15 hours a day.

A passage from his autobiography should hang in every classroom in America: "I have often reflected upon the new vistas that reading opened to me. I knew right there in prison that reading had changed forever the course of my life. As I see it today, the ability to read awoke inside me some long dormant craving to be mentally alive."

Malcolm X, his autobiography and his passion for reading continues to touch lives. Writer Sandra Cisneros says his life story is the book that has had the most impact on her.

"It was an awakening for me about my own race and class issues," Cisneros says. "It made me a revolutionary in a way. It affirmed the power of books to change the world because it had changed individuals like Malcolm, empowered him and, therefore, made him dangerous."

Malcolm was dangerous because he spoke the truth as he saw it and was tireless in pursuit of justice. What he would have done, how much more he would have grown had he lived, is fascinating to ponder but unknowable.

Time is better spent knowing the remarkable book that tells his story.

When T-Jeff meets Sally, again

5/16/1999

This weekend in Charlottesville, Va., marks the annual meeting of the Monticello Association, whose 700 members are the descendants of Thomas Jefferson. For the first time, descendants of Sally Hemings, the slave by whom Jefferson most probably fathered at least one child, were invited to attend. As guests, not family.

The ghost of Thomas Jefferson, haunting the grounds of Monticello, was listening to Lauryn Hill on my portable CD player and singing along.

"That thing/that thing/that thingggg," he warbled.

"Dang, T-Jeff," I said. "There haven't been this many black folk at Monticello since you had slaves."

He winced. Then a blue-haired society lady fainted as Madison Hemings V asked her to dance to Sly and the Family Stone's "Family Affair." Before passing out, she was heard to sigh, "Damn you, DNA!"

From the way he was closely examining the faces of his black descendants, marveling at the family resemblance, it was clear that the slavery issue was a very touchy thing with him.

As we walked, the voice of a woman humming could be heard coming from Mulberry Row, the slave quarters where T-Jeff's slaves lived nine to a room. Standing near an oak tree was a beautiful dark woman in a long yellow dress: the ghost of Sally Hemings.

As she approached us, T-Jeff swallowed hard.

"H-h-hello, S-Sally," he stammered.

"Wellll," she answered softly but strongly. "If it isn't Mr. All Men Are Created Equal and Endowed by Their Creator with

Certain Inalienable Rights and Entitled to Life, Liberty and the Pursuit of Happiness Unless of Course They're His Children by a Slave Who He Doesn't Free Until After He Dies and Then Never Frees Their Mother. Hello."

T-Jeff was stunned. "Gee, Sally," he said. "You sound a little angry."

"That is self-evident, Mr. Writing That Orangutans Prefer Black Women to Their Own Species Until He Gets an Unbearable Urge to Want to Lie Down with Me."

"All right! I messed up! I said and did some stupid things. I'm a two-timing hypocrite. But it's been 200 years. How long you gonna hang this over my head? Look! They're all here. All of your, eh, our, offspring are here."

Sally looked at T-Jeff with disdain. "Listen, Thomas. I want all your kin to accept all of our kin as part of the family, deserving of all the same rights and burial privileges as every other Jefferson. I put up with a lot of mess from you when we were alive, and I'm not going to put up with it in this afterlife."

"But I'm dead, Sally. What can I do?"

"You're gonna be worse than dead if I come back here next year and see things haven't changed. If you have to appear before every single one of those folks and scare them into doing right, you'd better do it." She stopped and disappeared.

T-Jeff stood with his mouth agape. Around him, white and black Jeffersonians were mingling.

"Don't worry, T-Jeff," I said. "Things will work out. Look at all your family getting to know each other."

"Yeah, I guess you're right. Maybe it's a new day," he said. "Say, ah, do you think you could introduce me to Lauryn Hill?"

"T-Jeff!"

"I play a mean violin."

"Forget it, T-Jeff."

Burying victims of another war

9/1/1999

On Sunday afternoon, the blue sky above San Fernando Cemetery was chased away by thick clouds riding a strong wind. An unnatural bustle rippled through the darkening cemetery as visitors hurried to pay their respects before the rain came. When it did, a string of cars with their headlights on, not unlike a funeral procession, poured out of the cemetery and into the street. A few people waited out the rain in their cars, but an older woman in a house dress and scarf sat on a marble bench under a tree in Block 27 as her male companion tended flowers at a nearby grave. Mother Nature has no respect for solemn remembrance; the rain and wind desecrated graves, tossing decorations throughout the cemetery—a pink heart emblazoned with "Mom" in the street near Block 3C; a large red bow between Blocks 39 and 40; a cross wrapped in purple ribbon between Blocks 39 and 36.

Unlike a cemetery across town, Fort Sam Houston National Cemetery, whose bleached-white headstones stand in uniform attention, the tombstones in San Fernando Cemetery are a mélange of sizes, colors and shapes. And yet in this cemetery, as in Fort Sam's, are the victims of war, tiny casualties of battles who didn't have to leave their country to die. Last week, the U.N. Security Council passed a resolution urging all countries to protect children during war and to stop turning them into soldiers. The history of war has been that of young men dying for the follies and vanities of old men. But in the 1990s, children have borne the brunt of battle. In the last decade, armed conflict has killed 2 million children, seriously injured or disabled 6 million, orphaned 1 million and made 12 million homeless. Another 300,000 children, ranging in age from 7 to 18, have been conscripted to fight in wars in Afghanistan, Sudan, Colombia and Sri Lanka. The United States isn't under siege from another country, and its children aren't being asked to fight old men's battles—and yet . . .

In Block 36 of San Fernando Cemetery lies Yvette Moreno in an unmarked grave that only a few people know exists. Twelve years ago on this day, the 5-year-old was sexually assaulted and beaten to death by her stepfather. She'd be 17 now.

In Block 37 is the grave of Mary Beatrice Perez, the 9-year-old who disappeared during Fiesta and was found murdered a few days later. Mary's picture is tied to a white plastic cross at the head of her grave, which is dotted with artificial red and white flowers and three small stuffed animals. A little silver windmill spins furiously in the breeze. Rain pelts the picture of the smiling girl. A windmill—this one large and pastel-colored—also spins at the well-adorned grave of Preston Dominic Huerta in Block 28. In May, the 7-week-old boy was beaten to death. Less than 10 feet from Preston rests Dominique Rodriguez, the 5-year-old beaten July 4. The decorations are gone, but on her bare dirt grave is a red ribbon blown from someone else's burial site. Perhaps a breath of remorse from Mother Nature. No bugle sounds taps for these soldiers, who fell in the war that was their lives. While rain slants in from the east and a breeze sprints through the cemetery, the only sounds are the chorus of birds and the tinkling of wind chimes tied to a tree near Preston's and Dominique's graves.

Somewhere, another grave is reserved for someone like them. Allison Cooke, a 5-year-old who lived in San Antonio until she went to her father's home near Dallas this summer. He's accused of beating her to death last Friday. In cemeteries throughout this land—a country that is not under siege and does not conscript its children into battle—more little battered bodies will rest. On this day, the sky stopped weeping and turned blue again. Storm clouds moved on. If only the war clouds would do likewise.

Coach's legacy is St. Gerard students

11/16/2005

On the last Friday night in October, after a football game at St. Gerard High School's Alumni Stadium, Coach George Pasterchick gathered his team in the southwest corner of the field near Rocky's Tree. It had been planted in memory of John "Rocky" Riojas, a 1982 graduate, former player and San Antonio police officer killed in the line of duty in 2001.

After a prayer, the players and assistant coaches ran to the locker room, leaving Pasterchick, a solitary figure in khaki pants and a blue pullover, walking down the sideline in that hitched gait of his, eyes fixed to the ground as if he were trying to remember every step and every patch of fading grass on what he knew would be his last trip to the locker room after a home game.

Sitting in bleachers emptying of parents and students unaware of the significance of that walk, I watched Coach from across the field and clapped for him, knowing hundreds more would have been there to applaud if they'd known that next week's game in Waco would be his last.

"It was very traumatic," he would say later, "knowing it would be the last time I'd be wearing that blue."

Last week, after 34 years as a football coach at St. Gerard, 32 of them as head coach, Pasterchick announced to faculty and students what he'd decided last summer: He's retiring, thus ending one of the most significant football coaching careers in San Antonio history.

It was a career that included coaching jobs with just about every semipro and professional football team in San Antonio during the last 40 years, a career that should take him into the San Antonio Sports Hall of Fame.

But most importantly, it was a career that touched the lives and ambitions of hundreds of students who came through the little Catholic high school on the East Side (of which I'm a member of the school council). Many of us are who we are today because this robust man with the bushy eyebrows cared enough about us to push, nurture, assist and inspire us into being what he knew we could be.

Outside of my family, no other person made a bigger difference in my life than Coach. Then again, when someone has known you since you were 14 and has played such a large role in your life, he is family. I'm just one of many for whom Coach has been more than a coach.

Many of us are asked about Coach when it comes out that we went to St. Gerard: "Is Pasterchick still there?" or "What was Pasterchick like?"

For most of this past season, I begged Coach to go public with the announcement that he was retiring so he could receive the grand and celebrated send-off he deserved. I even went through his lovely wife of 51 years, Maxine, but he refused, saying he didn't want to take any attention away from his players.

On Monday morning, Coach sat in his office and reminisced.

"It's unbelievable the kids who have come here," he said. "I never got up in the morning dreading to go to work."

That he's spent his last fall on a sideline hasn't sunk in yet.

"Am I doing the right thing?" he says he asks himself. "It's got to be time. How much longer can I go? I'll be 76 in September when the ball goes up in the air. I'd rather walk away than be carried away."

On Sunday morning, at a Mass at St. Gerard Catholic Church celebrating the life of Rocky Riojas, a man named Gil Candia shook Coach's hand and said, "You're a legend."

Is Pasterchick still there? Wherever he'll be, Coach will always be with us, the fortunate ones.

Nephew No. 6 can ask
about anything—except women

3/9/2002

Dear Zion (Nephew No. 6):

Welcome to the world.

I must admit that I was hurt when I called you Wednesday and you wouldn't come to the phone. Most people usually get to know me before they stop taking my calls.

But I felt better when your mother reminded me that you were only a day old and weren't yet able to use language properly. That's the same problem I have.

I'm sorry that your first few hours on earth were rough, but you've turned the corner; you are breathing easier and already have proven yourself to be a tough kid. You would be breathing even better if you weren't in Houston.

Because you were born Tuesday, you won't be able to read this now. I didn't learn to read until I was 11 days old.

Since Houston is your birthplace, my first gift to you is 35,000 shares of Enron stock. It's cheaper and more reliable than diapers and serves the same purpose.

I'd also like to offer you some words of advice that you will no doubt cherish and pass on to your own children.

Your mother is my sister, and you're her first child. As one firstborn to another, milk it for all it's worth. The things you can get away with . . .

Should anything happen to me before you and I can go into detail on this, there's a secret drawer in my nightstand which has a manuscript titled "I'm Number One: Things I Got Away With as the Firstborn."

Zion, always listen to your mother—unless your Uncle Cary

tells you something different. Besides God and your mother, I am the most important influence in your life. I am the dominant male figure in your life; I will shape you and steer you toward greatness. You can come to me for anything except money. For that you go to your other uncles and grandfather.

Always remember that you have a great and storied last name, one that's spoken in awe, revered and sought after by bill collectors throughout the southern part of the United States.

But since two-thirds of them will think your name is Clark, you won't have much to worry about. You apparently already know how to screen your calls.

You have a beautiful, biblical first name. It's the name of a great song Lauryn Hill wrote about her son of the same name.

Make people call you by your birth name and don't let them give you nicknames or shorten it to "Z" or "Zeester." Got that, Z-man?

Always remember that what a person earns isn't a measure of what they're worth and that there is dignity in any job as long as it's honest and you do it well.

But don't become one of those parking meter reader people who do their jobs so well that they give out parking tickets at 5:57 p.m. and are loathed by all who work and shop downtown.

Women? Being that I've not yet been able to convince one to stay with me for any measurable period of time, I'm not the least bit qualified to help you with this one. Go ask your mother for advice and come back and tell me what she said.

Lastly, Zion, whatever you do and wherever you go in life, always wash your hands. Preferably with soap. You can go a long way in life with clean hands.

Love,

Cary

P.S. Can you hurry up and get back with me on the woman thing?

Happy birthday to a brilliant thinker

11/25/2007

You're 11 years old, many springs ago, when you fall in love with baseball. And at that sweet spot in time, when you're watching the NBC game of the week on a Saturday afternoon, a commercial comes on promoting Major League Baseball. On the screen, with a voice-over, appear these words:

> Whoever wants to understand the heart and mind
> of America had better learn baseball.

> — Jacques Barzun

Those words intrigue and stay with you even though you're not sure what they mean because you're only 11. And that strange name also stays with you even though you can't pronounce it because you're only 11. From that moment forward, that sentence and that name will be wed eternally to your love of the game.

That sentence is now on a plaque in the Baseball Hall of Fame. Of the millions of words Jacques Barzun has written, of the thousands of lines he has elegantly crafted, it is the most famous and oft quoted. But in his astonishing body of work produced in his astonishing life, there are so many more to savor and reflect upon.

This Friday, Barzun, one of France's great gifts to the world, will turn 100 years old. As he reads this page of tribute this morning, in his home on the northeast side of San Antonio, he will insist he isn't worthy of such praise, but this man, who knows all there is to know about all there is to know, must know, despite his modesty, that such public acknowledgment of his life and the praise it naturally evokes is the very least that can be offered him.

90

Little in the 100 years of his life or the thousands of years of human existence has escaped him or the marvelous jewel that is his mind. As a historian, writer and educator, his legend was already secure before the 2000 publication of his magisterial *From Dawn to Decadence: 500 Years of Western Cultural Life, 1500 to the Present*. At the age of 92, he was a runner-up for the National Book Award in nonfiction.

The subjects he has written about extensively, passionately and knowledgeably include French and German literature, science, etymology, philosophy, psychology, art, race, education, crime fiction and, of course, baseball. He can discourse as easily on Michel de Montaigne, the 16th-century Frenchman who may have been the greatest of all essayists, as he can on Mickey Mantle, who may have been the greatest of all New York Yankees, Barzun's favorite baseball team.

Those who are infatuated with the mind-numbing tests that are dropped, leadlike, on students would do well to read some of Barzun's writings on testing, starting with *The Tyranny of Testing*.

Crime fiction hasn't had as enthusiastic and discerning a reader as Barzun, perhaps the only person who can detect in Archie Goodwin, Nero Wolfe's assistant, the failures of American foreign policy.

Each time he takes pen to paper the result is a clear and vigorous prose brimming with wit. The same grace that distinguishes Barzun's writing has always been reflected in the grace with which he's lived his life. In mannerisms, dress, speech and conduct, as well as writing, he has been a model of style and dignity.

And in not restricting his range of interests and giving his mind license to venture through centuries and across a range of subjects, he has also been a model of just how rich the life of the mind can be and how much it's a part of a rich and full life. He is an enormously generous man as well—at times, indulgent.

Nearly four years ago, that onetime 11-year-old was visiting with Barzun in the sunroom of his home. After discussing writing, satire, baseball, the war in Iraq and a discovery that Alexander Hamilton was the favorite Founding Father of both, there was a request that couldn't be stifled.

"Please," it was asked of the icon, "I've got to hear you say it."

With a smile and twinkle in his eye, Barzun said, "Whoever wants to know the heart and mind of America had better learn baseball."

And whoever wants to know the heart and mind of anything worth understanding had better learn Jacques Barzun.

Happy 100th birthday, Jacques.

Soldier's song ends in hymn

5/24/2007

It was supposed to be his songs that put Marquis McCants' name in the newspaper. Melodies and rhythms, beats and lyrics were to be the reasons eyes across the country would see his name in print and maybe, just maybe, praise his talents.

In his 23 years on this earth, Marquis, a 2001 graduate of O'Connor High School, got into the paper twice, but not for his songs. The first time was on a discordant note seven years ago when he was unjustly arrested. The second time, accompanied by a funeral hymn, was this Tuesday with the news that the specialist in the Army's 82nd Airborne Division was killed on his first deployment to Iraq. Marquis and 33-year-old Sgt. 1st Class Scott Brown of Windsor, Colo., lost their lives Friday when their unit was attacked.

Marquis was almost 17 in the summer of 2000 when his father, Savage, called me, upset that Marquis had been arrested in Alamo Plaza for jaywalking. Marquis was humiliated as he sat handcuffed on a bench and watched nine white people jaywalk without being arrested. As he recounted what happened by phone he was still stunned at his arrest.

When his father went downtown to pick him up, the senior McCants was surprised to see that about 20 youths, all black, had been arrested, a statistical oddity that led him to believe black youths were being targeted.

I called Al Philippus, the police chief at the time, who denied the assertion. But a few days later, after an editorial board meeting, he asked to see the police reports I had, took down their case numbers and two days later called to say mistakes had been made. He was apologetic and said he'd already put a stop to that.

What stayed with me most about that incident, along with Chief Philippus' initiative and candor, was Savage McCants' fierce passion to protect his son and clear his name.

Over the years I wondered what Marquis was doing with his life. I wondered until Monday afternoon when a colleague, Scott Huddleston, sent an e-mail telling me of Marquis' passing.

In August Wilson's play *Joe Turner's Come and Gone*, a character named Bynum says, "Everybody has to find his song."

Marquis McCants was in search of his song. He was in search of the songs through which he could express his thoughts and feelings, reveal a little of his soul and make a living for his family.

"He wanted to start his own production company," his father said. "He had a business sense about him and would help local groups."

McCants says Marquis didn't consider the military his first option.

"I didn't want him to go into the Army," says McCants, a retired Air Force master sergeant who served for 25 years. "He had a plan for his life."

Marquis' plan for when he got out of the Army was to get a degree and pursue a music career. Those are the songs he was in search of, and those are the songs that this God-awful war prevented him from capturing.

But know this: Marquis found his songs. Listen to how his father talks about him.

"He had the most loving spirit in the world," says McCants. "If you were down, he'd say something crazy to lighten the mood."

That's a song.

Marquis was a medic and, in a statement, one of his commanders said, "Specialist McCants distinguished himself by providing life-saving care on several occasions to members of the Red Falcons (his battalion's name) and the Iraqi people."

That's a song.

Marquis joined the Army to provide for his wife and three children, the oldest of whom is 3 years old.

"Everything he did was for those kids," said McCants. "He loved them to death."

That's a song.

Living your life with a compassion and love that graces the lives of your parents, your wife and children, your colleagues and strangers is a song that will resonate longer and deeper than any gold-selling record.

You sang well, Marquis. You sang well.

Bridging two cultures
in San Antonio easy as a youth

2/29/2004

The two longest streets, both stretching more than six miles, that connect the historically Mexican American West Side to the historically African American East Side are Commerce Street and a street with four names.

Beginning as Buena Vista on the west, it crests on a bridge before becoming Dolorosa and Market streets downtown and ending as Montana on the east.

As a native San Antonian, I've crossed the Buena Vista Street bridge hundreds of times.

As an African American living in a city that is predominantly Mexican American, I've crossed the bridge between African American culture and Mexican American culture all of my life, naturally and without thought that it was anything other than normal.

Growing up as a member of an ethnic group that was small in number and dwarfed by two other groups, I felt like the stepchild not invited to the ball. I felt an aching irrelevancy.

Yet even those feelings couldn't dampen my love for this city and its diversity.

I was raised to appreciate all people and cultures. If I'd been born and raised in Milwaukee, I'm sure I would have a special affinity for Polish culture.

But I was born and raised in San Antonio, and other than my own African American heritage, there are no other cultures that I embrace more, or feel more comfortable in, than Mexican American and Latin American. In both are a soul and passion absolutely necessary to my being.

Most of my neighbors on the East Side were black, but Latinos also lived among us. It was a neighborhood of both the middle class and the poor, of beautiful houses and some that were run-down. It was far from a slum or ghetto, but it says a lot about the mentality of my friends and me that, as children, we felt sorry for the rare white family that moved into our neighborhood.

We believed that no white family, if they could afford to do otherwise, would choose to live near us, those who were black and brown. That had to mean a huge fall from the paradise we imagined all white people lived in.

But they never stayed long, moving, we assumed, to someplace better.

On Saturday afternoons I could stand outside and hear both R&B and Tejano music. One block down the street was the neighborhood convenience store that was owned by a Mexican American named Joe, who lived in the back with his family.

But the first tamales I ate were bought three blocks down from the black-owned icehouse on the corner of South Pine and East Commerce, across from the Friedrich Building. They complemented the Mexican food my grandmother cooked every two weeks.

Except for first grade, all of my education came in integrated schools.

My oldest friend from those years is Charlie Puente, from second grade. As a child, my exposure to the home lives of people who weren't black came from my Mexican American friends, like Charlie, who invited me over to spend Saturdays with them and to sleepovers. I learned that their home life wasn't that different from mine.

I didn't relate to them as Mexican Americans, or them to me as African American. We were just kids with interesting stories to tell in different accents.

Today there are, at times, unspoken tensions between Mexican Americans and African Americans that I worry will erupt.

One reason is that blacks and browns can be just as prejudiced as whites. Bigotry is colorblind.

Another factor, perhaps larger, is that members of both groups sometimes make the mistake of fighting over small pieces of the economic and political pies, instead of working together to create more and bigger pies. Then there is the recent argument over the "status" of who is the country's largest minority.

My family is extraordinarily diverse and includes a Mexican American aunt; two cousins who are black and Mexican American; and a niece whose mother is Puerto Rican.

Because of my family, I live my life as if there are no walls separating me from people who have a heritage and history different from my own. I have much to learn from others, and they from me. I believe that's how a free and open child of the world should live, crossing the bridges into other cultures.

For it's in the crossing and re-crossing of these bridges that we keep them from crumbling.

Remember this name
when you go to vote

2/19/2008

There was never any doubt when you were in the undeniable presence of the Rev. James Orange. Whether he was leading a workshop on nonviolence, participating in a protest march or simply walking down Atlanta's Auburn Avenue, "Shack Daddy" couldn't be ignored. At 6 feet 5 inches tall, weighing more than 300 pounds and, in his younger days, resembling football star Rosey Grier, Orange was a civil rights giant in the literal and physical sense.

And while his name is in the pages of any good book about the civil rights movement, his presence never occupied a place in the popular imagination or culture of the country he loved and for which he was beaten, gassed and jailed in his lifelong crusade to make things better. With his resounding baritone, this gentle man also gave voice to the movement by singing freedom songs, such as "We Shall Overcome," "Ain't Gonna Let Nobody Turn Me Around" and "We Are the Ones We've Been Waiting For."

James Orange wasn't a household name, but his lifetime of putting his life on lines where his conscience led him will benefit households in Texas who begin early voting today for the presidential primaries.

His death at the age of 65 on Saturday in Atlanta came two days before the 42nd anniversary of his presence in a jail that ignited a train of protest that would run through Selma and Montgomery, Ala., and wouldn't be stopped until it got to Washington and President Lyndon Johnson's signing of the Voting Rights Act.

Orange, whose spirit and body was enlisted into the movement when he heard a sermon in the Sixteenth Baptist Church in his

99

hometown of Birmingham, Ala., was a young field staffer for the Southern Christian Leadership Conference when he ventured into Perry County, Ala., to organize. On the morning of Feb. 18, Orange was arrested for contributing to the delinquency of young people by encouraging them to participate in voting rights drives.

That night, amid rumors that he would be lynched, 400 people marched to the jail, where their plan was to sing a freedom song for Orange, but they were attacked by Alabama state troopers and police. Jimmy Lee Jackson, a 26-year-old activist, was coming to the defense of his mother and grandfather when a trooper shot him. His death eight days later led to plans for a march from Selma to Montgomery.

The first attempt for that march was on March 7 and became known as Bloody Sunday after state troopers prevented the activists, including Orange, from crossing Edmund Pettus Bridge by beating and gassing them. Later that month, Martin Luther King Jr. would lead the successful march from Selma to Montgomery that would lead to the legislation signed in August.

Orange became one of King's most trusted advisers and a man who believed in, lived and taught the philosophy and practice of nonviolence. When King took the movement to Chicago, Orange, writes historian Taylor Branch, won the respect of gang members by enduring nine beatings and telling them, "The people in the North are more beaten down."

Orange was in Memphis with King when he was assassinated, and in footage of the funeral procession he can be seen marching behind the horse-drawn casket. As an activist and as a regional coordinator for the AFL-CIO, Orange spent the rest of his years marching, organizing and teaching, whether in South Africa, where he traveled to train the African National Congress in voter registration before the release of Nelson Mandela, or in the streets of America, where he worked to wean gang members off violence.

The 1965 march from Selma to Montgomery for voting rights isn't that far from the 2008 presidential primary in Texas on March 4. Beginning today, voters will have two weeks to cast ballots paid for by the lives of Jimmie Lee Jackson, the Rev. James Reeb and Viola Liuzzi.

They were of a generation who moved America forward by taking it back to the spirit of the sacred documents that gave birth and meaning to the nation.

Orange was part of that generational wave of purpose and idealism that kept beating against the walls of resistance until those walls came crumbling down, and only because those walls came down do voters have a historic opportunity to vote for an American original like Hillary Clinton or Barack Obama to run for president against an American hero like John McCain.

There will be no holidays to celebrate his birthday or statues to preserve his image, but when voters cast their ballots they can honor James Orange by singing a freedom song to his memory.

Past disappears
with ice house's demolition

2/27/2002

In Monday's twilight, as a man driving by watched, a small boy wandered around a pile of fresh rubble on the corner of East Commerce and South Pine.

If the boy noticed the man he wouldn't have understood why he stared so hard at the rubble. But the day will come, years from now, when the child will understand.

It will be a day when pieces of his past, a place that was a landmark of his childhood, lie in ruins and he looks upon them with the same nostalgic gaze.

The bulldozing of the debilitated and abandoned structure, across the street from the Friedrich Building, was overdue.

It had been dead for years but wasn't buried until Monday. In the prime of its life it had been an ice house, the most convenient and happening ice house in Denver Heights on the city's East Side.

If many of the patrons knew its name, they never used it. In the '60s, '70s and '80s it was simply "the ice house," as in "I'm going to go get a beer at the ice house," or "There's a card game over at the ice house," or "Meet me at the ice house on the corner of Commerce and Pine," or "Momma, bring me something back from the ice house."

At the ice house, besides candy, chips, soda and beer, you could get some delicious tamales. For many of the children in the neighborhood their introduction to tamales was through the ice house.

They also sold sausage that was good, but not nearly as good as the sausage you could get over at Johnny Johnson's on Montana and South Olive.

After picking up some tamales or sausage, you could go two stores down on Commerce and get some moon cookies at the largest mom-and-pop store in the neighborhood.

In the ice house, you could sit outside or in a small room where you could eat and drink or play cards or dominoes while the jukebox played the best of Motown and Stax as well as James Brown, Sly and the Family Stone, Aretha Franklin, Al Green, B. B. King, Gladys Knight and the Pips, and Bobby "Blue" Bland.

The music may have been loud and the lyrics sometimes suggestive, but parents didn't have to cover their children's ears because of any vulgarities.

When the 5 o'clock whistle at Alamo Iron Works sounded, everyone in the neighborhood knew workers there as well as some of the people from Friedrich would gather at the ice house to down a few.

To be sure, some spent too much time at the ice house, ignoring their families while blowing their money and wasting their lives on drink.

Sometimes there were fights and sometimes the police had to be called, but mostly people went to the ice house to have a good time, especially if they didn't have money or transportation to go anywhere else.

The ice house even got a little national attention in the late 1980s when it was mentioned in a *New York Times* story that proclaimed San Antonio the ice house capital of the world.

But the world and neighborhoods change. In 1993 the ice house closed. On Monday it was demolished.

The boy walked away from the rubble.

The man drove away from his past.

2008 campaign will reveal
America's racial tolerance

11/16/2006

Should he run for president in 2008, Barack Obama will do what Colin Powell declined to and invite the nation to cross into unexplored territory of its racial landscape.

It's either a mirage or a signpost of maturity, but in all of the talk about Obama running for president it's remarkable how little race is mentioned.

It's as if the question of whether America is ready for a black president has been dismissed and the national conversation is solely about the reasons to vote for Obama or the reasons to vote against Obama, none of which has anything to do with race.

But until that ground is crossed and broken, the question will remain unanswered.

Jesse Jackson's 1984 and 1988 presidential runs were historic and revivalist affairs that were the most serious campaigns by a black candidate to date. For a fleeting moment in 1988, after he'd trounced Michael Dukakis and Al Gore in the Michigan Democratic caucuses, Jackson scared the Hades out of the Democratic Party graybeards with the possibility that he might actually win the nomination.

Jackson's campaigns were heroic but never had a chance of propelling him to the White House. The only African American who ever loomed as a formidable frontrunner and a prospective presidential candidate was Powell, who decided not to seek the Republican nomination in 1996.

More so than Jackson, Powell would have made the nation ask if it was ready for a black president and, possibly, would have earned an affirmative answer.

Can an African American be elected president?

Call me an optimistic fool, but I believe the answer is yes.

True, Harold Ford Jr. may have lost his race for the U.S. Senate because of a racist campaign ad. Still, a 36-year-old black man nearly got elected to the Senate from Tennessee.

Ford and Michael Steele, the black Republican nominee in Maryland for the Senate, may have run the year's two best Senate campaigns, and in a year when "R" wasn't such a politically deadly scarlet letter, Steele probably would have won. What's more, Massachusetts elected a black man, Deval Patrick, governor.

It says a lot about where we are as a nation that the frontrunner for the Democratic presidential nomination, Hillary Clinton, is a woman, and the potential candidate generating the most excitement, Obama, is a black man. Were she not tainted with the Iraqi war, Condoleezza Rice would be an ideal candidate for the Republicans.

New York Times columnist David Brooks, a conservative, has written, "The next Democratic nominee should either be Barack Obama or should have the stature that would come from defeating Barack Obama."

In Tuesday's column, I downplayed the criticism about Obama's lack of experience because I believe that experience is an ambiguous commodity and that the quantity of years in elected office has never been an accurate barometer for the quality of a presidency.

If the biggest argument against an Obama presidency is his "inexperience" and not his race, that's a measure of progress. A presidential campaign will magnify his gifts and flaws but shouldn't highlight his race.

It's by the content of his campaign that we'll be able to judge if Barack Obama is just a comet flashing across the horizon or an enduring star ready to take his place in the political constellation.

Bettas can be fine pets;
just don't go on any trips

8/16/2004

The circumstances of his death will, again, cast suspicion on me. Any minute now, I expect the authorities to come knocking on the front door of the Clack Cave to take me in for questioning.

I know it looks bad, but I didn't kill the fish.

A couple of years ago I wrote about being the prime suspect in the mysterious death of my betta, Juan Negro Blue, who died in my apartment while I was on a business trip.

He was a gift to me from a family in the Valley. My initial dislike for the fish, including "forgetting" to take it out of the car the first night and "forgetting" to not put it in water with chlorine, which could kill it, was eventually overcome, and I gave his name much thought.

"Juan" because he was given to me in San Juan; "Negro" because he had some black in him (and with Africa the Motherland, all of us have some black in us); "Blue" because he was mostly blue.

Being black and blue made Juan a biracial betta. Being black and blue also inspired his taking up the harmonica and recording an album titled *Mo' Betta Blues* after a Spike Lee movie starring Denzel Washington.

I don't know how Juan died. Honest, I don't. But I ended that column proclaiming my innocence and vowing to buy another betta in his memory.

I did. In fact, I bought one almost identical to Juan and named him Juan Negro Blue II.

When I returned from a trip last weekend, Juan Negro Blue II was at the bottom of his bowl, deader than the Texas Democratic Party.

Two bettas in my care, two business trips, two strange deaths. But I didn't do it.

Still, I panicked and, looking for a creative way to dispose of the body, I went to my neighbor Frank, the alleged ax murderer, who may or may not have experience in such matters.

Frank wasn't home so I flushed Juan II down the whirling porcelain tunnel. An autopsy would have proved my innocence, but if I'm being framed, I wasn't taking any chances.

I've learned a lot about bettas over the past couple of years, with the possible exception of how to take care of them. But I tried and I fed Juan II every day and regularly cleaned his bowl when cleaning it wasn't an inconvenience. I decorated his bowl with a plant and some multicolored glass rocks—rocks that I will now glue to rings to give as gifts to those special someones.

If there's one regret I have it's not getting Juan II a companion. You can't put two male bettas together because they will fight, charging at each other and attacking and biting the other's fins until they are tired.

Not unlike the presidential race.

On the other hand, you can put female bettas in together and they get along just fine, and you will often see two of them going off to the ladies' room together.

I thought about getting a female betta for Juan II. But one of the betta Web sites had this warning: "Mating bettas is not an easy task and should never be tried 'just for fun.'" (If you're mating bettas "just for fun," you have serious issues.)

My innocence is bolstered by the fact that the average life span for a betta is two years. Juan II simply ran out of gas, not unlike this column.

Like Juan I, Juan II is gone, and I've now been banned from pet stores.

On the road to New York

A flashing road sign on I-81 North in Harrisburg, Pa., is a blinking testament to understatement.

"Major accident. Avoid New York City."

What happened here was no accident.

The term "major accident" doesn't explain the view Wednesday evening from the New Jersey turnpike into Manhattan: a gaping hole where the twin towers of the World Trade Center once majestically stood.

Now a plume of thick, white smoke spirals from the rubble across the blue sky.

On the long journey from San Antonio to New York, it was obvious that too many people cared about what happened here for it to have been just an accident.

Outside Waco, two people placed a message on a sign outside of a church, asking for prayers for the country and our president.

In a Nashville convenience store, a young clerk with Elvis-like sideburns and shades asked incredulously: "What happened? I just don't understand this."

Along a dark Tennessee highway, flashing signs read: "Americans are proud" and "We'll repay."

Throughout the almost 2,000 miles, American flags could be seen at half-staff, hanging limply and sadly.

In Virginia, flags were placed on telephone poles as clouds hung low, etched against the Blue Ridge Mountains.

The world as we know it ended Tuesday.

The two airliners that destroyed the World Trade Center not only changed the geographic landscape but also forever altered the nation's psychological and emotional landscape.

For mornings to come, we will wake wondering if what happened has truly happened.

We will pinch ourselves, shake our heads and look at each other, eyes agape, because doing such things, we think, will wake us from the nightmare.

We will imagine that we're actors in a Bruce Willis movie or characters in a Tom Clancy novel or unwitting players in a hoax like Orson Welles' *War of the Worlds* radio broadcast.

But this is real.

The world as we know it ended Tuesday.

Not because of a loss of innocence. People who live in a nation that has survived a great Civil War, assassinations of presidents and the Oklahoma City bombing lost their innocence long ago.

We're in the early hours of a horror too immense for our minds to comprehend and too heartbreaking to fully fathom.

Tuesday on National Public Radio, a young woman being interviewed was frantic to get home to her 2-month-old daughter.

"Will there be a tomorrow?" she cried. "Will there be a future for my baby?"

Never before in this nation's glorious but tumultuous history have these questions yielded such uncertain answers.

In the days to come, we'll continue to live through some of our worst fears. But we'll also be reminded of our goodness, our generosity, our heroism and our resilience.

We'll be reminded of something we often forget: that we are one people and one nation.

We'll be reminded of our power to rebuild that which has been destroyed and to bind wounds that have been opened.

On Wednesday evening, the last standing section of the south tower of the World Trade Center collapsed, giving birth to a fresh plume of white smoke that could be seen from the turnpike.

The flashing road sign said New York City is to be avoided.

More than ever, it should be embraced.

Families of missing
find bond amid hope
···

NEW YORK, 9/14/2001

A city of 8 million people is haunted by the thousands missing.

Amid the incessant noise, chatter and rush of New York City, a pizza parlor on the corner of 6th and 11th streets may be among the most solemn of places.

Ray's Pizza has become a kind of clearinghouse for the missing.

On the outside window and wall of the small eatery and on a light post in front of it, families and friends have posted fliers asking for information about lost loved ones.

All have been missing since Tuesday morning. All worked in the World Trade Center.

Giovanna "Gennie" Gambale was last seen on the 105th floor.

Kevin Williams on the 104th.

Venesha Richards on the 100th. Nural H. Miah and Shakila Yesmine, a couple, on the 93rd.

Saying little, clusters of people stare at the pictures with reverence before moving on.

"Let's hope they have a future," a man said to his wife and children.

About a block down the street, on the corner of 11th and Greenwich Avenue, some family members of the missing carry that hope, along with photographs, as they stand outside St. Vincent's Hospital.

These families speak to each other in "floors," as in: "What floor was he on?"

"The 91st. What floor was your sister on?"

"The 102nd."

Among them is the family of 62-year-old Anthony Luparello Sr., who was last seen on the 101st floor.

His son, sister, son-in-law and daughter-in-law held his picture for all to see as they waited for news of his fate.

"On Tuesday, I went to see if my father got out, but the building collapsed and I had to run for my life," says Anthony Luparello Jr.

Incredibly, the father and son were working in the World Trade Center in 1993 when it was bombed.

They both escaped unharmed, but this time . . .

"It's getting harder," answered Luparello when asked if he believed his father was still alive. "We're just hoping, but no one is telling us anything."

The family believes the elder Luparello's selflessness may have cost him his life. During the 1993 bombing, he helped people to safety.

"He's the kind of person who'd stay in the building to help other people," says his daughter-in-law Dorothy.

She recounted Luparello's last conversation with his wife Tuesday morning as he witnessed the destruction of the first tower.

"He was crying hysterically on the phone when it hit the first building. 'People are jumping out of the building! They're killing themselves!' "

Over the phone, his wife yelled for him to get out.

"It's not my building!" he screamed. "But people are killing themselves!"

This missing man's son, clutching his father's picture to his heart, is asked if he's angry.

"That comes later on," says Anthony Jr. "We just want whatever they can find, any kind of people, survivors . . . hoping . . . hoping."

Heavens open up
and weep over New York

NEW YORK, 9/15/2001

In a poetic tribute to the end of a sorrowful week, the weeping of this part of the Earth was emulated by that of the heavens.

The national day of prayer, remembrance and mourning called for by President Bush commenced with a thunderstorm.

Before sheets of rain swept across the city a little after 1 a.m., strong gusts of wind blew through Times Square.

While an American flag snapped violently in the wind, leaves and a piece of newspaper chased each other in circles nearby on Broadway, spinning as ceaselessly and madly as the world has for Americans since Tuesday.

On Friday, they sought respite from the spinning with the anchor of their faith, whatever—if any—that may be, and a shared humanity with others that transcends faith, race and nationality.

Eleven o'clock on Sunday morning has been called the most segregated hour in the United States, a time when ethnic groups worship only among themselves.

But when the bells began ringing from the Church of Saint Mary the Virgin, an Episcopal Church on West 46th Street, the pews were filled with the glorious diversity that is New York, the United States and the world.

The noon Mass at the church is daily. The purpose for Friday's service—joining houses of worship across the nation to commemorate the worst terrorist attack in its history—isn't.

"We had 15 people yesterday and we thought we'd get 30, 40, 50 people today," an amazed Rev. Matthew Weiler would say later. "But there were at least 400 people here."

Most had never been in this church before, and some were unfamiliar with the liturgy.

Two young women, perhaps Ethiopian or Somalian, got up and left during Communion only to return a few minutes later.

"Is the service over?" the taller one asked in a lilting voice.

When told no, that it was Communion, she smiled shyly and said, "Oh, we saw the people get up."

Not all worshipers were Christian.

"I'm Hindu," answered a man when asked if he was a parishioner. "But this is not a day about religious differences. It's a day about being one people."

In his homily, the Rev. Stephen Gerth, rector of the Church of Saint Mary the Virgin, spoke to those in the pews who lost loved ones in Tuesday's attacks.

"Your heart is already broken, but the rest of us are going there too. The enormity of evil hasn't hit us yet," he said. "I think it's going to be harder next week than this week when the *New York Times* is thicker because they print the names of the dead."

A rendition of "America, the Beautiful" elicited tears from men and women.

And when "Amazing Grace" was played, one couldn't help thinking of those still missing in the rubble a few miles away as people sang the words "I once was lost but now am found."

But of the many words said and sung before the children of the Earth left the church and went out into the street where the heavens still wept, perhaps none meant as much as "Peace be with you."

New York chaplain dies
doing what he was best at

NEW YORK, 9/16/2001

On Tuesday morning, a young Franciscan friar from St. Francis of Assisi Church was walking down Sixth Street when he saw a plane flying low, toward the World Trade Center.

Seconds later, he saw smoke coming from one of the Twin Towers and ran to his church and into the office of the Rev. Mychal F. Judge, the beloved chaplain of the New York City Fire Department.

"Father, I think they're going to need you at the World Trade Center," the young friar said.

The 68-year-old priest with the reputation of always going where the action was left immediately for what had become ground zero of the worst terrorist attack on American soil.

As Judge got near the towers, he encountered Mayor Rudolph Giuliani, who told him, "Pray for us."

"I always do," said the chaplain before rushing into the building with the firemen.

Minutes later, while giving last rites to an injured firefighter, Judge was killed when debris from the crumbling building fell on him.

Several firefighters, some of whom he'd ministered to for years, saw the collapse. There could be no rescue.

In the midst of the chaos, they gently lifted his body from the rubble and carried it to a nearby church, where they placed it in front of the altar and covered it with a sheet. They paused to place his fireman's badge on top of the sheet, then rushed back to the towers.

After telling the story of his courageous friend and mentor's final moments on Earth, his eulogist and friend, the Rev. Michael Duffy, said, "He's now my hero."

On Saturday morning, Judge was serenaded with bagpipes as thousands of mourners, including U.S. Sen. Hillary Rodham Clinton and her husband, former President Clinton, gathered in and outside St. Francis of Assisi Church on West 31st Street to say goodbye.

Before services started, a firefighter entering the church saw a friend standing in line.

"Vinnie, how are you doing?" asked the firefighter.

"Fine," answered Vinnie. "But how are you doing?"

"I had a whole building fall on me and all I got was a cut nose," said the firefighter, who had a button-sized scar on the bridge of his nose. "I was in Tower 1 on the 44th floor."

During his eulogy, Duffy said Judge couldn't and wouldn't have chosen a better way to die.

"He was where the action is. He was praying and talking to God and he was helping someone."

Judge's body was the first removed from the World Trade Center wreckage. The numeral "1" is listed on his death certificate, the first of thousands that will eventually emerge from this massacre.

For now, his family and friends are among the few to have been blessed with certainty as to the fate of their loved one and the recovery of remains.

During his funeral, fellow priests gave Communion to mourners in the street.

Communion in the street. Perhaps this good man would relish the irony that what killed him and thousands of others created exactly that across the nation: communion in the streets.

This couldn't have been what Osama bin Laden had in his demented mind.

Remembering the lost,
seeking return to normal

Were it not for the white clouds seen sliding across the blue sky from the corner of Church and Canal streets, it could have been a perfect Sunday morning.

But the clouds came from the still smoldering ruins of the World Trade Center.

A few blocks south of this corner, smoke could also be seen in Washington Square Park, but this was the smoke of incense perfuming the air around a makeshift memorial to the victims of Tuesday's attack.

Fliers of the missing were kept company by flowers, flags and candles along a fence surrounding the marble arch that dominates the park.

The fence was draped with canvases on which hundreds of people wrote messages.

On a day when no football games would be played in the nation's stadiums, 3-year-old Alex Alifonto cradled a miniature football in his arm as he crouched next to his mother, who was crouching to write the word "Soham."

"It's Sanskrit for 'I am that thou art the highest,'" Nicole Alifonto said.

Alex then pointed to a tall building and asked, "That one?"

"No," she answered. "He keeps asking if that's the building that fell down."

The memorial inspired a respectful and solemn quiet, which was anointed by the tears of those overcome with grief and longing.

But just a few feet away, in a playground, the laughter of children was a reminder that an almost perfect Sunday morning in a beautiful park should be a time of joy and not mourning.

Alex, the boy who knew that a building fell and did horrible things to people, just wanted to be a 3-year-old when he told his mother, "Let's go." He then led her to the playground.

A playground of excited giggles, thrilled squeals, squeaking swings, large stone turtles, slides, balls, balloons, sand and snacks under elm trees that leaned protectively over them.

And while the children played, a 25-year-old Brazilian man-child flew a kite.

Wearing cargo pants and a camouflage T-shirt, Marcel (no last name given) unfurled his kite some 200 feet over the park, making it wiggle and dance in the sky.

"Tuesday was big disaster," he said. "I don't like it. I like peace. I love this country. Maybe my kite makes people feel good."

Near the memorial, a man talked on a cell phone about the funeral arrangements for a friend who'd been killed Tuesday.

But his voice was drowned out by the singsong voices from the playground.

On a day when not a single touchdown pass would be thrown in the NFL, Alex laughed and ran as he threw his football into a tree, no longer asking which building fell down.

There are a thousand things to do on a near-perfect Sunday in New York City.

But on this Sunday, in this time, few are better than sitting on a park bench under a sheltering elm while listening to the laughter of children.

Trying to remember how it used to be.

Nuclear winter brings out
the new boys of summer

NEW YORK, 9/18/2001

It's Monday morning, and people are in a hurry.

Throughout the city, more streets, expressways and bridges are open, and trading has resumed on Wall Street for the first time since the destruction of the World Trade Center.

Today is the day everyone returns to work, and on Eighth Avenue they walk briskly to do just that.

They stride with purpose until they get to Eighth Avenue and 48th Street, where their gait slows until it comes to a complete stop. There, they look at a corner where it appears every flower in New York City has bloomed.

This isn't a magic garden. It's a fire station. Engine 54, Ladder 4, Battalion 9, to be exact.

As if on cue, two fire trucks with large yellow bows on their grilles return to the station.

They're applauded and cheered by those returning to work, people who've just been reminded that there are some who never stopped working and others who died on the job.

The firefighters and police officers of New York are the city's new idols.

In a souvenir store down the street, New York Yankees shirts have been placed inside the store while NYPD and FDNY shirts are prominently displayed outside.

In sporting goods stores, those shirts and caps as well as some from the FBI hang next to the No. 2 jersey of brilliant Yankees shortstop Derek Jeter.

But the celebration and celebrity of New York's finest and bravest have come at a terrible cost.

More than 400 of them have been killed or are missing since Tuesday. To replenish the officers' ranks, 168 "battlefield" promotions were given to firefighters in an emotional ceremony in Brooklyn on Sunday.

Here at Engine 54, the hundreds of flowers, votive candles and letters and drawings from children commemorate the 15 firefighters from this station who remain missing.

The smiling faces of men like Paul Gil, Joe Angelini and John Tippens are encased in a large frame under the words "Our Brothers."

Phil Seelig, who's been a firefighter for 10 years, says he can't yet comprehend the loss of his friends.

"Just about every firehouse in this battalion lost a lot of men," the 36-year-old says. "This is incredible. The worst fatalities the Fire Department had before now was 12 in the 1970s. So this is just unreal. It's just unreal. It looks like a nuclear winter with 4 inches of dust everywhere. And the debris itself, where the buildings were, is eight stories of steel, cement and Sheetrock."

As he talks, an elderly man approaches and silently shakes his hand.

"Thank you," the shy Seelig says.

He says the attention is embarrassing, but "it makes you realize people appreciate what you do."

He laughs when asked about the possibility that there are now some children who would rather be Phil Seelig than Derek Jeter.

"It's certainly more realistic to become a firefighter than a professional baseball player," he says.

Then, glancing at the pictures of his "brothers," he goes back to work.

Time, like terror, won't stand still

NEW YORK, 9/19/2001

Tuesday morning in Times Square at 8:45, people stopped what they were doing and said nothing.

One week ago at that time, New York City and the country were three minutes away from being horribly and permanently changed.

Knowing what we now know, that the first of two hijacked planes was minutes away from crashing into the World Trade Center, it's understandable if people want to go back a week so they could hold on to 8:45, freeze it and extend it into eternity.

If we could, there would be fewer jitters.

Tuesday morning, a young Chinese man in town for a cultural fair got on an elevator on the 33rd floor of the Marriott Marquis. When the car descended with a quick jolt, the man grabbed his heart and said: "I'm scared. This is scary. Everything scares me here."

His fear was so palpable and raw that others on the elevator felt sorry and then embarrassed for him.

In the streets, the screams of sirens, part of the aural landscape of any major city, now draw the attention of people who will follow the destinations of fire trucks and police cars with their stares before lifting their gazes to the sky.

"It's weird," a man tells his wife. "When you hear a siren in New York, you usually don't blink."

If 8:45 last Tuesday morning could be preserved, nearly 6,000 more people would be safe and accounted for, and the city wouldn't be caked with so much melted wax from the thousands of candles flickering in their memory.

If 8:45 could have held off 8:48 last week, Elissa Cinquemani's daughter wouldn't be a recluse, and John Halliday could still count on the generosity of a woman whose name he never knew.

Cinquemani carries with her a flier of Daniel Crisman, who was on the 96th floor of one of the towers and hasn't been seen since. Crisman is the boyfriend of her daughter, Danielle.

"Their life was going to be wonderful," an impassioned Cinquemani says.

She's out looking for Crisman because her daughter is too distraught.

"She won't leave the house. The one time she left was to get his dental records," she says. "I need to do whatever I can for my daughter."

Halliday raises money for the United Homeless Organization, asking passers-by to drop some money into the large water cooler-like bottle that sits on a table on 5th Avenue.

While donations have been down the past week, "people are still hurting," he says.

Until last week, he set up his table near the World Trade Center. Three weeks ago, a woman began making a daily contribution.

"Every day she would give $5, but I haven't seen her since the day before it happened," he says. "If I don't see her soon, I'll know she was in the building. Last night on TV I saw a woman who's missing who looked just like her, but I don't know."

Last Tuesday morning, the time of 8:48, like the evil it brought, wouldn't be denied.

Writing last week's wrongs

NEW YORK, 9/20/2001

By noon Wednesday, a pair of city workers were scraping melted candle wax from the steps of Union Square Park.

"Just don't touch the words," I wanted to tell them. "As they were written, there shall they remain."

Out of the rubble of what was the World Trade Center have sprung the flags that drape New York City, the flowers that scent its air and the candles that light its nights.

But even more prolific are the written words telling the story of its pain and what it means to so many.

Sidewalks, streets, store windows, cars, mailboxes, fountains, trees—just about everywhere people have taken up pens, chalk and markers to articulate their responses to the terrorist attacks.

We're all writers at heart. But most of us never take the time to hone the craft, and many simply avoid doing it.

Yet at certain times in our lives when we're moved by a great pain or joy, each of us has sat down to compose something that attempts to make sense of our feelings and thoughts.

Rarely, if ever, has there been a time in this country when so many had feelings and thoughts that demanded they be made sense of.

Never have so many people felt the need to do it so publicly.

Dipping their pens in the inkwells of their hearts, they're giving words to the unspeakable while trying to understand the incomprehensible.

Written language is the bridge they use to cross the solitude of their feelings and connect with others.

If journalists are writing the first draft of this post-9/11 history, people in the streets are sketching out the emotions of the time.

In Washington Square and Union Square parks, one trips over the messages written on the grounds in different hues of chalk.

On 42nd Street, windows are plastered with hundreds of messages on index cards.

The notes and messages are written to the deceased, their families, the nation, Osama bin Laden, the world.

They quote Frank Sinatra's "New York, New York"; Bob Dylan's "Blowin' in the Wind"; Marvin Gaye's "What's Going On?"; John Lennon's "Imagine"; and Lynard Skynard's "Freebird."

Passages and verses from the Bible, Talmud and Koran are cited, and people are urged to pray.

The messages are written by adults and children. They're written in English, Spanish, French, Hebrew, Arabic, Chinese, Italian.

People speak for their native lands in voicing their support for the United States. "Germany sympathizes with America," reads a sweatshirt. "L'Afrique pleure/Africa cries," says an index card.

There are pleas for peace ("Save the Human Race"); forgiveness ("I dare you to forgive"); anger ("Bush, strike back" and "Nuke 'em"); and humor ("Let bin Laden fight Mike Tyson for every New Yorker and American").

One note, written on an index card on 42nd Street, may still speak for most: "I don't have a message—I'm speechless."

Afghan immigrants forced to prove their citizenship

NEW YORK, 9/21/2001

While restaurants all over New York City have American flags in their windows, most restaurateurs don't feel the need to post a letter to "our neighbors and fellow New Yorkers" expressing their horror of the attack on the World Trade Center and extending their condolences to all affected by it.

But that's the kind of letter posted outside of the Afghan Kebab House on 9th Avenue.

Like several other Afghan restaurants across the city, this place has received threatening phone calls and accusations that the owners are terrorists.

Never mind that the owners have been in this country more than 20 years and are U.S. citizens, or that in this location, as well as the one on 46th Street, there are photographs of the owners with Mayor Rudy Giuliani.

At the 46th Street restaurant Tuesday, a young waiter—before being instructed not to talk to the media—said: "People find out we're an Afghan restaurant and leave. Some of our old customers haven't been back."

While I was dining at the half-full restaurant Wednesday night, a couple came in.

"Oh! This is an Afghan restaurant?" the woman asked, a realization that stopped her and her male companion in their tracks. "Do you think it's patriotic to eat in here?"

"Probably not," the man said before spotting something on the wall.

"Look, there's the American flag!"

So they stayed and ate.

While people outside lingered or did double-takes at the restaurant's name, one waiter nervously paced from the back of the restaurant to the front, looking outside.

A similar and understandable nervousness was evident Saturday afternoon at the Islamic Cultural Center when a Canadian television crew, a Columbia journalism student and I attempted to interview Muslims on the sidewalk as they came for a worship service.

A man rolled out of the mosque, a flag flying from the back of his wheelchair, and asked us to leave, saying we were on private property.

When we told him we were on the sidewalk, which is public property, he insisted that we leave. When a policeman intervened and told him we had a right to be there, the man returned to the mosque.

The policeman was there for good reason. Police are investigating 10 anti-Muslim assaults reported to have occurred over the weekend.

And it's happening across the country. A prime example of this bigotry is Frank Roque, a man accused of shooting to death a Sikh gas station owner in Mesa, Ariz., and firing at a Lebanese clerk and into the home of an Afghan family.

"I'm a patriot," Roque declared upon his arrest. "I'm a damn American all the way."

His perverted sense of what being a patriot and an American is contrasts mightily with that of Haider Alam, a cab driver—and Muslim—from Bangladesh who's lived in New York for nine years.

"I've volunteered to help and provide free transportation for the families who lost people in the World Trade Center," he told me proudly. "It's our duty, right?"

Profound message in simple greeting

NEW YORK, 9/22/2001

They say you can find anything on 125th Street in Harlem. I found a sage named Osgood.

With more than 6,000 people victims of the attack on the World Trade Center, New York City is plastered with missing-people fliers.

But this one, posted in a convenience store window, was different. A 12-year-old boy named Tiras Segreda has been missing since Sept. 9, making this the first missing-person flier I've seen in 10 days that does not concern the World Trade Center destruction.

As I turned to walk away, I saw a black man with a cane, maybe in his 70s, standing on the sidewalk, silently extending his hand to people who ignored him.

He was a solidly built 6-footer with gray hair, a thick gray mustache, a faded New York Yankees windbreaker, faded green pants and blue tennis shoes.

As I approached him, I reached in my pocket to give him some change. But he shook his head and said: "I don't want your money, son. I don't want anybody's money. I just want to shake your hand."

Dang, a freak, I thought. But I shook his hand.

"Shake a hand, make a friend," he said.

"Those are the last lyrics in Donny Hathaway's song 'This Christmas,'" I said.

"That's right," he said, "Those towers came down because too many other walls don't come down. We got to shake hands and make friends before we all fall down."

Alcohol was on his breath and his eyes were bloodshot, but I liked his way with words. He told me his name was Osgood but wouldn't offer more than that, even where he was from.

"It don't matter where I'm from—it's where we're going, son," he said. "People in pain are going to be in more pain if we don't do like Brother Hathaway said. Shake a hand, make a friend. I know you got to go, but let me walk with you a bit."

Despite the cane, he walked quickly. He pointed to the Adam Clayton Powell Jr. State Office Building and said he'd attended a candlelight vigil there Thursday night.

"I wish they'd hang Ladeen (Osama bin Laden) from the telephone post the way they did Mussolini when they got rid of him," Osgood said. "He got no business killing my people like that."

"Your people?" I asked.

"Look at all those countries those people who got killed came from. Those are my people. Those are your people too," he said, shocked that I didn't understand that.

I turned on Lennox Avenue. Osgood was going to continue down 125th.

"Goodbye, son," he said with a gap-toothed smile. "Remember to shake a hand and make a friend."

"Merry Christmas," I answered.

A couple of blocks down on Lennox, I saw a painting on an abandoned building that made me think of Osgood. A black girl smiles under the words: "My community is where my people are."

You can find anything on 125th Street. Including wisdom.

Baseball helped take
New Yorkers' minds off terror

NEW YORK, 9/23/2001

You knew it right away.

After the game-winning home run had sailed into the center field night just to the left of the flag at half-staff; after a wave of celebratory joy washed over more than 41,000 people who hadn't felt that emotion in more than 10 days; after the game had ended and this same joyful throng stood and sang "America, the Beautiful" along with the recorded voice of Ray Charles; after they left for home, not feeling this happy since the twin towers of the World Trade Center still stood; after this, you knew that baseball and other sports matter.

Baseball and major outdoor sporting events returned to New York City on Friday night when the New York Mets opened a three-game series at Shea Stadium with the Atlanta Braves.

The game wasn't played so that people could forget the unforgettable events of Sept. 11 but because life, gingerly and painfully, must go on. Also, because distractions from those events—however fleeting—are healthy.

It was just a baseball game, one in which people praised and criticized the season many players are having and speculated if the San Francisco Giants' Barry Bonds could hit 71 home runs.

It was a baseball game that mattered in the race for the National League East title as the Braves fade and the Mets surge.

It was a baseball game in which people could forget their fears and heartbreak, especially when Mets catcher Mike Piazza won the game with his two-run homer in the eighth inning.

Yet all around were reminders that it wasn't just a game:

the 20 flags flying atop the stadium at half-staff; the flags and posters that fans brought professing love of country and for each other; the outpouring of affection and thanks for rescue workers, firefighters and policemen; the moment of silence in a packed stadium in which the only sound was the fluttering of the American flags.

It was more than a regular Mets games because a noted Yankees fan, New York Mayor Rudolph Giuliani, received the loudest cheers of any individual as he marched from the Mets dugout to his seat behind home plate to the raucous chant of "Rudy!"

And when the announcement came that the first pitch would be delayed 10 minutes to allow everyone to get into the stadium, it wasn't greeted with boos but with cheers from fans who wanted their fellow New Yorkers to be a part of this memorable event.

Memorable it was.

There was no forgetting that 15 miles away, what used to be the World Trade Center was a graveyard of rubble for more than 6,000 people.

Friday night's game won't resurrect a single one or cease the mourning for them.

But for a little while people were able to laugh and feel good again. Outside Shea Stadium, a young black man played "God Bless America" on a trumpet while an older white man danced a jig.

The No. 7 train back to Manhattan buzzed with excitement and rolled with laughter as Mets fans talked about Piazza, not bin Laden, and thrilled at the prospect of another subway World Series with the Yankees.

These were people who didn't want to let go of the night and didn't want to release its joy because they know that we have many joyless nights ahead.

Lifting every voice
to honor those who fell

The rivers of the world flowed into the ocean of Yankee Stadium on Sunday afternoon.

They carried with them the cultures, languages and faiths that have nurtured the multicultural roots of the United States for centuries.

The colors of the flag that draped and filled the stadium were red, white and blue, but the people who came were black, white, brown, yellow and red, all the colors made by a creator called by different names by those there.

In the most hallowed of baseball parks, the ghosts of Babe Ruth, Lou Gehrig, Joe DiMaggio and Mickey Mantle lingered, but it was the spirit of others that was felt and remembered.

On Sunday, the statistics that mattered weren't the Babe's 714 home runs, Gehrig's 2,130 consecutive games played, DiMaggio's 56-game hitting streak or the Mick's 560-foot home run.

The numbers that were important were 6,453 and 261, representing the people still missing in the violated ruins of the World Trade Center and those confirmed dead, respectively.

It was for those victims, their families and the nation that people gathered for an interfaith memorial service. It was a large-scale version of the daily and nightly prayer vigils that have taken place throughout the city since Sept. 11.

The service wasn't just a memorial for the dead but a reminder to the living that a strength of this nation is its diversity and that religion shouldn't be an obstacle in creating community.

Mindful that at least 62 nations lost people in the attack and that an assault against one member of the human family is one against humanity, actor James Earl Jones thundered that what happened was an "unprovoked attack on every race and nation."

"We are united not only in our grief but in our resolve to make a better world," Jones said.

Rabbi Marc Gellman said 6,000 people didn't die that day but that "one person died 6,000 times."

"The death of each and every one would be worthy of such a gathering and such a grief," Gellman said.

Religious leaders of all faiths counseled for all to be wise and compassionate toward each other, yet there was a reminder of the intolerance and ignorance that threatens many.

Because some members of the Sikh faith have been mistaken for Muslims and harassed as such, some of the more than three dozen Sikhs sitting in the bleachers felt obligated to hold signs that read "Sikhs Love America" and "Proud to be an American and a Sikh."

One man wore a button that said, "I am a Sikh," with "Sikh" in bright red letters in case anyone thought otherwise.

No Sikh, Muslim, Christian or Jew, no one, should have to prove they're more American than the next person.

One's politics and faith weren't important Sunday as people shouted "U-S-A."

They did so in different accents but with one voice.

And when the Boys and Girls Choir of Harlem sang "Lift Every Voice and Sing," the Negro national anthem, more than three dozen Sikhs stood up and proudly waved their U.S. flags.

"We Shall Overcome"
inspires another generation

NEW YORK, 9/25/2001

On the first Friday after the worst Tuesday in this nation's history, New York City was in song.

At a candlelight vigil to remember the victims of the World Trade Center attack, thousands of people came together in Union Square Park, which had already become a gathering place for a young, pro-peace crowd.

Among the songs they sang were "God Bless America," "The Star-Spangled Banner" and "This Land Is Your Land."

Later that night, at a memorial erected for firefighters on Riverside Drive, there was a smaller candlelight vigil attended by an older crowd.

Among the songs they sang were "God Bless America," "The Star-Spangled Banner" and "This Land Is Your Land."

New York City has become a city of choirs, of sorrowful strangers coming together to sing in public. Perhaps at no other time have people been so moved by an event that it's brought them together in this way.

And on that Friday night, it was as if the people at the two vigils were singing from the same songbook.

The attack on the World Trade Center led to the re-emergence of another meaningful song, one that defined an important era in American history.

"We Shall Overcome," the anthem for the civil rights movement, is now being sung with a frequency and fervor not heard since the '60s.

It's always been a standard at African American and civil

rights–related events such as Martin Luther King Jr. holiday celebrations.

Now there are red, white and blue signs declaring, "We the people shall overcome." A New York television station adopted "We Shall Overcome" as its motto. At Sunday's interfaith prayer service in Yankee Stadium, people stood and locked arms as they sang the old spiritual along with the Boys and Girls Choir of Harlem.

One of the most moving moments came when a male soloist, in a strong and defiant voice, sang the stanza "We are not afraid" to a chorus of cheers.

An eloquent statement of purpose, the song doesn't deny the existence of evil in the world. It doesn't say "We Will Eliminate" or "We Will Eradicate."

It says, simply: "We Shall Overcome."

Once an anthem against an evil that would deny justice to American citizens of a particular ethnicity, it's now an anthem against an evil that would deny life to all Americans.

The song's truth is both in its words and in the strength of those who lift their voices to sing it.

A day to pay tribute and a day off

....

This morning, as he does most mornings, 72-year-old Lucky Ruffell will leave his home in the South Bronx and catch the subway to Battery Park in Lower Manhattan, carrying a saxophone case.

At the park, he'll sit on a stoop a few feet from the rippling, emerald green Hudson River and the ferries that take passengers out to Ellis Island and the Statue of Liberty.

If it's a sunny day, as it has been for the past few days and as it was a year ago, the sun's reflection will give the impression of thousands of silver coins dancing on the water.

This morning, as he does most mornings, Lucky will pull out the weathered 1948 Martin saxophone he bought for $125 and begin to play.

But today's performance will be special, because, as he said, "I'm playing for the people."

"The people" are the victims of last year's terrorist attacks, and while they are being honored officially by thousands just a few blocks away at ground zero, Ruffell will honor them the way he knows best: with music.

He'll play songs like "Misty" and "Somewhere Over the Rainbow" as well as some of his own improvisations. And today he'll add some special ones.

"Oh, I'm going to play 'America, the Beautiful,' 'The Star Spangled Banner,' 'Amazing Grace' and 'When the Saints Go Marching In,'" he said as he wiped his face with a handkerchief. "It's for the people."

Last year, on this morning, Lucky wasn't at the park playing his saxophone by the river. He wasn't there when one of the hijacked planes, American Airlines Flight 11 from Boston, soared across the Hudson and brought death when it crashed into the north tower of the World Trade Center.

In his office on the 85th floor of the tower that morning was Bill Forney III, a Houston native who is a commodities trader for SMW Trading Co.

Amid ash, flame and darkness, Forney and co-workers somehow escaped.

This morning, unlike that morning, Forney will take the day off.

"All of this has been tucked away in the back of my mind," said Forney, 28. "It's only recently, seeing more and more of this in the media, that's bringing back the memories. Very strong and vivid memories."

He doesn't have nightmares, he says, but some things are different.

A few days ago, while watching television in the Upper West Side apartment he shares with his wife, Tobey, he heard an airplane.

"It had a high-pitched scream that scared me to death," he said. "I muted the TV and waited to hear the worst."

Forney isn't sure how he'll commemorate today.

"I'd like to go to the site (ground zero) and be in it, but I'm sure they won't let me do that. I'm not sure what I'm going to do."

Except for being cooler, the forecast for Lower Manhattan today is the same as it was one year ago: sunny and beautiful with clear skies. It's ideal for the solemn ceremonies that will mark the anniversary.

And perfect for a man with an aged horn sitting by the Hudson River, alone, and screnading the people.

Let there be justice, joy on earth

12/21/1997

Paper snowflakes, decorated with a child's coloring, adorned the windows of an eighth floor hospital room in Santa Rosa's Children's Hospital. A person admiring the snowflakes last Sunday morning would have seen a silver balloon drift past the windows and over the large Christmas tree in Milam Park, becoming a disappearing star in the southeastern sky.

'Tis the season when dreams are given full flight, set loose across the horizons of our imaginations toward a destination consecrated by faith.

'Tis the season when that homeless child named Hope, so often shunned throughout the year, finds temporary shelter in the manger of our hearts.

'Tis the season of wonder and cheer, of silent and holy nights, of jingle bells and halls decked with holly.

'Tis also the season when we are reminded that we are a better people than we give ourselves credit for; that our capacity for love and generosity is infinite, limited only by imagination and will. It is this season, more so than any other, when our obligation to each other is more clear.

So it must also be the season when we ask ourselves why the Christmas spirit of cheer and giving isn't extended the year round. Aren't the other seasons of our lives worthy of such gifts?

Let there be peace on earth, but let there also be justice, for without it peace is shallow and uncertain.

Let there be goodwill toward all men, and women, but let it be deepened with understanding and appreciation.

Let there be joy to the world, but remember that the world includes the dispossessed, the despised, the afflicted and the neglected. For 'tis the season when we remember a young and wandering family who were shunned as they sought refuge. Let us resolve to always find room for those who wander across our lives seeking whatever comfort we can offer.

Let us also resolve that we will be more vigilant in not allowing our homes and souls to be invaded by ignorance and fear.

Let there be no room in the inn for hatred. Let there be no room in the inn for prejudice. Let there be no room in the inn for injustice.

In all, let there be no room in the inn for anything that diminishes the individual and engenders bitterness.

Let there also be fun as we throw ourselves into the merriment of flashing lights, brightly wrapped packages, sugar cookies and eggnog and the warmth of family and friends.

For 'tis the season when we marvel at the magic in our lives and the magic of life itself. The miracle of life. It is a precious thing, so easily taken for granted.

And, in this season of miracles, let's pray that life is enjoyed fully by all, including the child with the window of paper snowflakes.

May all our dreams and prayers, like silver balloons ascending to the heavens, find their way home.

To each of you I wish a Happy Hanukkah, a Merry Christmas, a bountiful Kwanzaa and a joyous New Year.

Happy birthday to a legend

1/16/2007

I don't have a mark on my face, and I upset Sonny Liston, and I just turned 22 years old. I must be the greatest!

—Cassius Clay in 1964

I won the title, became champion. Powerful and strong. And then God tries you, takes my health. Fixes it so it's hard to talk. Hard to walk. I'm blessed and thankful to God that I understand he's trying me. This is a trial from God. He gave me this illness to remind me that I'm not No. 1; He is.

—Muhammad Ali in 2001, speaking to National Public Radio about having Parkinson's disease

He was 12 when he predicted, in rhyme, to the *Louisville Courier-Journal* that he would win his coming fight; 18 when the international community first took notice of him with his gold-medal performance in the 1960 Rome Olympics; 22 when he upset the Mike Tyson of his era; 25 when he took on the U.S. government and popular opinion; 28 when he was allowed to return from exile and practice his craft; 32 when he whipped George Foreman to regain the title; 54 when he made the world gasp as he dramatically appeared from the shadows of a Georgia night to light the Olympic torch to commence the 1996 Summer Olympics.

On Wednesday, Muhammad Ali turns 65. No athlete of any time or era has occupied a larger cultural presence, consumed more attention, stirred larger controversies and evoked more love and hate than Ali.

Had he just been a boxer of unsurpassed physical gifts, one who transformed an inherently brutal sport into ballet and art, he would still be a memorable figure—one whose personality, beauty and athleticism would have made him, behind Babe Ruth, this nation's most mythologized athlete.

But because he unwittingly became a symbol of black pride, youthful rebellion, opposition to the Vietnam War, and individual conscience, only Jackie Robinson trumps him as the most socially significant athlete in American history.

Parkinson's hasn't slowed his mind, but it has slowed his movement, put a stolid mask upon his once expressive face and made that famous voice inaudible. Still, he may be the most recognizable and certainly one of the most loved figures on the planet.

Which isn't to say many in this country still don't hate him. Ali's refusal to be inducted into the Army transformed him into something more than an athlete and, along with his earlier embrace of Islam, a reviled figure.

Ali tested the allegiance of many other Americans to the value of principled dissent and the right to worship as you choose. He even tested the simple right for a person to be called by the name they choose to be called. People who had no problem calling Marion Morrison "John Wayne" or calling Archibald Leach "Cary Grant" refused to call Cassius Clay "Muhammad Ali."

There are many legitimate reasons why someone would dislike Ali, and his stance on Vietnam is one of them. But the biggest lie against him is that he was a coward.

Ali knew he would not have been in threat of seeing combat had he accepted induction. He rejected a deal from the government that would have let him fight exhibitions, defend his title and continue to earn a substantial income.

He didn't flee the country but had his title stripped, wasn't allowed to fight for three and a half years, went broke and was prepared to go to jail when the U.S. Supreme Court ruled unanimously in his favor in 1971.

He took the hardest legal punch his government could hit him with and stood his ground with the same dignity with which he fights Parkinson's.

I'm an unapologetic fan of Ali's, aware of his flaws but understanding that, like most of us, his virtues are greater.

My favorite Ali story is when he was training in Pennsylvania for the Foreman fight and a father brought his 12-year-old son, Jimmy, to see him. Ali asked the boy why he was wearing a skullcap, and the boy told him he had leukemia and had lost his hair. Ali told Jimmy that he would beat the cancer and Ali would beat Foreman.

A few weeks later, when the boy was dying in the University of Pennsylvania hospital, Ali went to see him and reminded Jimmy that Jimmy would beat cancer and he would beat Foreman.

Jimmy looked at Ali and said, "No, Muhammad. I'm going to meet God and I'm going to tell him that you are my friend."

That says it all. Happy birthday, Muhammad Ali.

Amadou, it was never about you

....

3/1/2000

Makes me wanna holler and throw up both my hands.

—Marvin Gaye, "Inner City Blues"

What were you thinking, Amadou? Why did you do it?

Why did you make four New York City police officers fire 41 shots at you, hitting you with 19 of them?

It was your fault, they said, during the trial that acquitted them of all charges. If you hadn't been skulking around and acting suspicious before pulling out your wallet, they'd have never opened fire on you.

Who did you think you were, little brother? Thinking you had a right to stand in the doorway of your apartment building, a free man in a free land, an innocent man in a not-so-innocent land.

How dare you, Amadou Diallo, not know the fear you evoked in the four menacing men in plain clothes who approached you that night, men who may or may not have identified themselves as police officers?

They said they did, but they said a lot of things that may or may not be true. They lived to tell their version of that night, which they now say was a horrible mistake. We heard them talk, and we saw them cry.

But we didn't hear from you, Amadou, though we did see your mother cry. And we saw others cry, those who couldn't believe a verdict that meant no one was accountable for your death. Except you, of course.

No justice, no peace? No justice, no surprise.

Your voice was silenced, Amadou. Who speaks for a 23-year-old West African immigrant who peddled goods 12 hours a day six or seven days a week? Who speaks for the man who had the audacity to believe in the American dream and the desire to work for it?

Lady Liberty, standing in the New York harbor, beckoned you, Amadou. She seduced you with the words, "Give me your tired, your poor, your huddled masses yearning to breathe free."

Who did you think of, Amadou, when you huddled in your doorway, in fear for your life? How free did you feel when the first of the 19 bullets tore through your body?

You didn't journey here from Guinea to become a martyr, did you, Amadou? You didn't struggle so you would become a household name not because of the way you lived but because of the way you died.

Why, Amadou? Why did you make them do it? They were only doing their job.

Don't you know it's your fault for not being white? An assumption of innocence was never given to you. You were indicted by the color of your skin and convicted and executed by fear and panic.

But Amadou, if you'd been white and slaughtered in the same way, the questions wouldn't stop. Race may explain why you were a suspect, but it doesn't explain the acquittals of your killers. After all, the jury of your peers included four black women (though defense attorneys attempted to remove three of them with peremptory challenges).

This trial was never about you, Amadou. It wasn't about your fear, your perceptions and what went on in your mind that night. It was all about the policemen and their fears, their perceptions and what was going on in their minds.

See, you didn't scare them to death. You scared them into causing your death.

Mistakes do happen, but mistakes should never be worth a life.

And more than anything, Amadou, this is what makes so many people of all ethnicities and colors want to holler and throw up both their hands: The world has been told that four police officers who shot an innocent and unarmed man 19 times aren't legally responsible for his death.

One of the policemen, the one who fired 16 shots at you, said that as you lay on the ground he held your hand, rubbed your face and begged you not to die.

But you did anyway. Why did you have to die, Amadou?

Look at all the trouble you've caused.

If I were a spy—
and I'm not saying I'm not

4/23/2005

It was reported last week that the ultra-top-secret government spy organization, the National Security Agency, would open an office in San Antonio and create 1,500 jobs. Having a certificate of completion from the Maxwell Smart School of Spy Masters, I called the NSA to inquire about a job.

The phone rang eight times before a man answered.

"Hello."

"Good morning, is this the National Security Agency?" I asked.

"Who wants to know?"

"I do."

"Why?"

"Listen," I said, "is this the National Security Agency or not?"

"What if it is?"

"I'd like to apply for a job."

"How did you get this phone number?"

"I called information."

"What information?"

"The operator?" I said, getting impatient. "411. Are you or aren't you the National Security Agency?"

"If we were—and I'm not saying we are—but if we were the, what is it you called it, the National Security Agency? What is it that you want?"

"I told you that I'm interested in applying for a job."

"Where?"

"Here in San Antonio."

"What makes you think we're in San Antonio?"

"It was in the news. You're opening an office at the former Sony plant."

"We are? I mean, they are? Oh. What kind of job are you interested in, that is, if this were the National Security Agency and we were hiring?"

"Well, I'd like to come in and discuss with someone the different opportunities that will be opening up there."

"I'm sorry, but that can't be done. If this were the National Security Agency, it wouldn't be possible for you to talk to anyone employed by the agency unless you were already employed by the agency."

"What? Then how does one apply for a job? How does one get interviewed if one doesn't get to talk to the people in the National Security Agency who are doing the hiring?"

"We have our ways."

"We?"

"I mean, if this were the National Security Agency—and again, I'm not saying it is—I'm sure they would have their ways."

"Has the National Security Agency always been like this?"

"Sir, first, you may be wrong in your assumption that there even is a National Security Agency."

"But I read it in the paper."

"Sir, do you believe everything you read in the paper?"

"One of them. Look, the National Security Agency does exist, doesn't it?"

"Maybe it does and maybe it doesn't."

"Come on! You were created by President Harry Truman in 1952."

"Sir, I can't confirm or deny that."

"That it was created by President Harry Truman in 1952?"

"Sir, we can't confirm or deny that a President Harry Truman ever existed."

"What?"

"Nor can we confirm or deny that there was ever a year called 1952."

"This is crazy. Just tell me how to apply for a job there."

"No need to apply, sir. If we were the National Security Agency, and I'm not saying we are, we already know everything about you. Everything."

Picking up the pieces
of shattered justice

The Statue of Liberty greets me as I drive into Tulia on U.S. 87. She doesn't know that Tulia scares me more than Jasper.

Say the name Jasper and the image of a screaming man being dragged to his death on a dark East Texas road is pulled across people's minds.

Mention Tulia and it's likely to invoke little more than a furrowed brow and vacant gaze. If its significance is known, it's doubtful anyone will associate it with the Statue of Liberty. Yet she salutes me with her torch.

It's actually a green and weathered 6-foot replica of the statue that stands in front the Liberty Suites hotel. She was there June 16 to welcome Freddie Brookins Jr. and 12 other defendants who returned home on a bus after spending years in prison for crimes they didn't commit.

It's why they were taken from their homes that Tulia scares me more than Jasper. Not the tiny town itself, hidden in the Panhandle between Amarillo and Lubbock. With its brick streets and more than two dozen churches, Tulia is an economically depressed town with closed and boarded-up businesses. At 10 o'clock on a Friday morning, its pulse is hardly livelier than at 10 o'clock Sunday night.

Nor is it the people of whom I'm wary, people who are polite and who easily shake your hand and engage you in conversation.

Tulia scares me because this community's tragedy of people arrested, convicted and sentenced for things they didn't do could just as easily happen to me. Or you. And it's more likely to happen than a motorized lynching.

Values we hold dear to our national soul, enshrined in our laws and engraved on our public conscience—civil liberties, the presumption of innocence, fair trials—were shattered in Tulia, and it's now up to this farming town of less than 6,000 to pick up the pieces.

The danger of picking up broken pieces is in cutting yourself, but Tulia has been cut enough and already has bled too much.

Tulia is Spanish for "destined for glory." But Tulia's name is a mistake. When it was settled in the 19th century, it was supposed to be named after nearby Tule Creek, but a misspelling changed its name. The mistake has outlasted the now anonymous man who made the clerical error.

With fortune and reflection, Tulia's name will outlast that of Tom Coleman, the strange and devious man who did so much to tarnish its name and the names of its citizens. In another town, by mistake or malice, the tarnished name could be mine. It could be yours.

The people of Tulia can't be blamed for bringing Coleman into their midst. The fault lies with those who hired him as an undercover agent for the Panhandle Regional Narcotics Trafficking Task Force, despite the soiled reputation he'd earned in previous law enforcement jobs.

Nor can the people of Tulia be blamed for the infamous pre-dawn raid on July 23, 1999, in which 46 Tulians, 39 of them black, were arrested. That raid led to 38 of them being sentenced to prison with no evidence that Coleman actually made the drug buys from the defendants that he claimed.

On Aug. 22, Gov. Rick Perry issued pardons to the defendants. Coleman has been indicted on three counts of perjury.

What the people of Tulia must ask themselves is why so many of them were willing to believe the worst about fellow citizens with whom they'd lived for years. Why would they take the word of a stranger who had lived among them for only 18 months?

Like Jasper in its moment of infamy, Tulia deserves the opportunity to search its soul for answers. When I visited Jasper on Easter weekend in 1999, between the trials of the men who murdered James Byrd Jr., I was impressed with people's willingness to understand how this crime could happen in their community and to talk openly about it. Blacks and whites admitted to working harder at a civility they'd taken for granted, but the most powerful comment I heard came from Willis Webb, publisher and editor of the *Jasper Newsboy*: "We all have to ask ourselves, what little have I done that might have contributed to this—that allowed this to happen."

Last month, I visited Tulia. Before my trips to both Jasper and Tulia, there were warnings from friends to be careful. The warnings were both playful and serious, but had I been white I doubt anyone would have been concerned about my safety.

I understood. Race played a role in both crimes. I'm a black man. Most of the Tulia defendants were black males. Many people, including Jeff Blackburn, the Amarillo attorney who was the lead defense counsel for all the defendants, believe that the drug sting was an attempt to get blacks, about 8 percent of the town's population, out of Tulia.

Tulia scares me more than Jasper because the threat of physical violence doesn't frighten me nearly as much as the possibility of being falsely accused and convicted of something I didn't do and having people believe the charges.

The brutality in Jasper and the injustices in Tulia were so egregious as to transcend race. In Tulia, especially, what happened isn't simply an example of one rogue lawman turned loose on one community, but of what can transpire when people become lax in safeguarding their constitutional rights and liberties. What happens when they neglect to assume responsibility for neighbors whose rights and freedoms have been violated?

In Tulia, it doesn't matter now what Vicki Fry's ethnicity was when she was wrongfully arrested. What's important is that a woman who was seven months pregnant lost her baby days after her arrest.

I'm not one of those who sees the government as a demonic entity dispatching agents in black helicopters to burst into the homes of law-abiding citizens and ferry them away in the darkness. Still, that's what happened to Freddie Brookins Jr.

On the morning of the raid in Tulia, Brookins was sleeping when his wife woke him to tell him someone was knocking on the door of their duplex. He wrapped a bedsheet around himself and went to the door. When law officers brought him out of the house, they stripped him of the sheet, revealing his nakedness in front of bright lights and television cameras.

"Kids and everybody were outside," Brookins says. "Every corner you looked at, they (law enforcement officers) were running into houses."

Now 26, Brookins spent 3½ years in prison for something he didn't do. On the jury were people who'd known him since he was a child. "Everyone in the jury, I knew," he says. "One guy was my basketball coach when I was a kid. I spent the night at his house, even as a teenager. His boys have spent the night with me. This man knew me, and he still convicted me."

Inside Rip's Country Grill, Brookins walks by an older white man who shakes his hand and talks to him for a couple of minutes. "That's Darrell Stapp," he says. "He's good people."

Near the Swisher County Archives and Museum on Southwest Second Street, I met a white woman who'd served on one of the juries. She says she reluctantly voted to convict one of the defendants. But that was before she knew about Coleman's duplicitous and criminal past.

"I'll never serve on a jury again," she says, not wanting her name used. "Not if it's going to hurt people."

Alan Bean, a Methodist minister in Tulia who helped publicize the plight of the "Tulia 46," believes that once the hurt caused by the sting operation is acknowledged, the town can move forward.

"Anytime that you can get people on both sides of the issue to sit down at the table, it's positive," says Bean, referring to conversations now taking place. "If we can change the economic development instead of who was right and wrong about Coleman, we're putting it behind us."

In the Jasper City Cemetery, the grave of James Byrd Jr. has a metallic tomb in which someone, an entire town even, can see his or her reflection.

There is no similar monument in Tulia on which people can pause to reflect, only the faces of living men and women and the pain they're trying to get over. Only when all of Tulia's citizens see each other and the promise of a future together will they bridge that pain.

When that's done, it will no longer be symbolic that the Statue of Liberty standing in front of Liberty Suites has her back to the town.

Let's cheer for the underdog

2/9/2006

Little Birdy, you won't be forgotten. Others may laugh at your final moments and cheer your demise, but not me. A half-ton bull flying into the stands may not be a sympathetic figure, but I understand you.

I'm the guy who watches the original *King Kong* and cheers for Kong. What did he do so wrong that it should cost him his life? He was an ape with a glandular problem living in his homeland when strangers came, captured him, drugged him, chained him, made him the star of a freak show in New York and then killed him because he got upset. Before Kong is even caught, I pull for the ridiculously stereotyped "natives" to send the intruders back to where they came from.

And just what was that whole kinky interspecies thing with the woman?

But no one speaks up for Kong and tells his story. And no one is speaking for Little Birdy, or Pajarito, the 1,108-pound bull who got tired of being played with in a Mexico City bullring. The video shows Little Birdy, or Birdy to those of us who support him, suddenly racing across the ring and leaping into the stands.

Birdy cleared a wall and a second, higher fence in the most amazing leap made by a bull not named Michael Jordan. He landed on spectators and pushed himself through the crowd, injuring but not killing any of them.

Sadly, one of the matadors followed Birdy into the stands and stabbed him to death.

Again, as with Kong, what did Birdy do so wrong that he deserved to die such an untimely and brutal death?

You take a dangerous, hot-blooded animal and tell him he has to work on Sunday, have some guy in tights and a funny hat tease him by waving a red cape in front of him, daring him to attack, and you don't think the bull is going to get ticked?

He's a bull. He's single, he's a stud, he wants to be sowing his wild oats instead of listening to some show-off shouting "Olé."

Not to mention the name. Little Birdy? This is one of the baddest animals on the planet and they name him Little Birdy? He deserves a name that resonates with courage and virility, like Hulk or Cary.

So Birdy had enough.

In defending Birdy, I make the same defense that Chris Rock used for the tiger that attacked Roy of Siegfried and Roy. People said the tiger went crazy, but Rock says, "The tiger didn't go crazy. The tiger went tiger!" And Birdy went bull.

Some will ask about the poor innocent people who were injured and frightened when Birdy charged into the stands, but they were cheering Birdy's humiliation and waiting for him to get killed so they could cheer louder.

And you know how fans are. We don't know what they were screaming at him. They could have been talking about his mama, saying that his woman was with another bull, saying he should be performing with Siegfried and Roy—we just don't know.

But we do know that Birdy didn't have to die. For years, the Green Bay Packers, especially the receivers, have celebrated touchdowns by doing the Lambeau Leap and jumping into the stands. If they were killed every time they did that, Brett Favre would have no receivers to throw to. Maybe Birdy just wanted to show his love for the fans. Then again, maybe he was sick of life, knew what would happen to him by going into the stands and committed suicide by leap.

We'll never know. But Birdy, we will work for the day when giant apes and bulls will no longer be killed because they're giant apes and bulls.

Time to obsess about washing, not obsessing

....

7/23/2006

When the Edwards Aquifer Authority announced last week that the drought had forced it to impose Stage 1 water restrictions on the region, they forgot to issue this critically important note: Water Restrictions Do Not Mean You Wash Your Hands Less to Conserve Water. Please Wash Your Hands.

I would hate for this omission by the authority to undermine my modest mission to get people to wash their hands EVERY TIME they visit the restroom, cover their mouths when they sneeze or cough, play with their dogs or scratch their scalps.

In a pre-Thanksgiving column last year, silly me thought it would be a healthy and civil activity if people would wash their dirty hands before shaking cleaner ones or putting their filthy hands on food that others will eat.

After the column ran, a friend of mine told me, "I'm guilty. I don't always wash my hands. Your column made me realize I need to do better."

My first thought was, "Man, I've eaten at your house. Now you tell me you don't wash your hands?"

So I've got this thing about washing hands. But I've got to talk about a book.

There is a third-floor hallway here at the paper that I traverse to get to my office. The hallway is lined with filing cabinets, boxes and bookshelves and stacked with books. For a few months now, one book has repeatedly caught my eye.

The book is titled *Overcoming Obsessive Thoughts*. I can't stop thinking about that book.

Each time I walk by its stack I have to look at it, gaze upon the red letters on the white and brown background and make sure it's still there.

There are times throughout the day when *Overcoming Obsessive Thoughts* crosses my mind. I wonder if I ever cross its pages?

Published by New Harbinger Publications Inc. in 2005, the book was written by Christine Purdon, Ph.D., C. Psych., and David A. Clark, Ph.D., L. Psych.

I find myself thinking about Dr. Purdon and Dr. Clark, wondering how they met, do they hang out together and would they like me. I wonder if they wash their hands after going to the restroom.

On Thursday, not wanting *Overcoming Obsessive Thoughts* to be long out of my view, I brought it to my office to examine it closer.

Dr. Purdon dedicated the book to Mary and William, and Dr. Clark dedicated it to Natascha and Christina. I wondered who Mary, William, Natascha and Christina were and if they washed their hands. I wondered how Natascha got her name.

But the thought that stays with me most is that to devote the time and research to write a book titled *Overcoming Obsessive Thoughts*, doesn't one have to be obsessed with it?

I wonder if that thought ever crossed the minds of Dr. Purdon and Dr. Clark.

And now that I'm holding their book in my hands, I'm wondering who held this book before me and where their hands had been.

Excuse me, but I have to go wash my hands.

San Antonians' goodness
far exceeds caller's venom

9/10/2005

You have all of these monkeys coming here from Louisiana. You be sure to house them on the East Side because we don't need them on the South Side, West Side or North Side. All these dumb (expletive) who didn't know how to clear out for a damn hurricane, we don't need them here.

This city is going to give them housing when we can't even take care of our own. This city is just like the United States. We can't take care of our own, but we take care of everyone else in Iraq, Iran and Afghanistan. And now we've got more (expletive) monkey (expletive) (expletive) coming to this town.

Prepare for more (expletive) trouble in this damn town with crack, prostitution and crime and hopefully you'll keep it on the damn East Side. You have a good day. Peace out, nigger.

—Phone message from a caller named Nathan on Tuesday

Dear Nathan,

When I called you on your cell (caller ID, bro) and identified myself and asked if you'd called, you hesitated, said I had the wrong number and hung up. (That happens often when I return calls like yours, of which I get many.) When I called back I got your voice mail (that's how I got your name).

Later you left two messages in which you admitted making the calls and requested to speak to me as one San Antonian to another and said that everyone is entitled to his opinion. You uttered no profanities or epithets in those messages in a tone that was more civil but said your only request was that I not print your name or phone number in the paper.

You left me with the impression that you didn't want people to know the language in which you expressed your opinion.

I made two good-faith attempts to call you, but you lied the first time I did and didn't pick up the second time, so anything you want to say to me will have to be face to face. But relax, I'm not printing your number, last name, place of employment, Social Security number or favorite cereal.

I'm one San Antonian who has never been more proud of his city than when we welcomed the victims of Hurricane Katrina. It's a response that confirms my belief that people are essentially good and will help others in need.

Yes, a few of those fleeing from Louisiana are thugs. But just as you wouldn't want to be defined by those toxic comments of yours, no group of people wants to be defined by its minority that's a criminal element.

Most of these people you call "monkeys" who stay here will become hardworking and productive San Antonians.

Out of these human beings you call "monkeys" could emerge a doctor who may one day save your life or that of your child.

Most of these children of God you call "monkeys" would open their hearts to you if, God forbid, you suffered a similar tragedy. They'd try to ease your pain without passing judgment or casting aspersions, just as many San Antonians, of all colors, are trying to ease theirs.

You see, Nathan, there's an instinct in people that's stronger than bigotry or hate. It's love. Sometimes, in tragedies like this, we have to be reminded that the best things we have going for us—and what will be our salvation as a species—are love and our obligation to each other.

You're entitled to your opinion, but in this case—and I've never said this to anyone—I speak for far more people than you do.

Peace,

Cary

An eerie reminder
of Mississippi's plight

Studded across this small coastal community are sets of steps that go nowhere.

They ascend into air or to what's left of a floor. To stand on one of these strange steps and gaze south is to see a sight that's not strange at all.

On the other side of U.S. 90, a family of three plays on a beach whose sands spread out into the Gulf of Mexico. Above the gulf's dark and gently rippling waters, seagulls soar and dive under a light blue Sunday sky that's topped with swirls of whipped cream-like clouds.

But in Long Beach, as in towns and cities along Mississippi's Gulf Coast, there are steps leading to nowhere.

On Aug. 29 of last year, Hurricane Katrina made a devastating and deadly sprint across the coastlines of Louisiana, Mississippi and Alabama.

Katrina is forever linked with New Orleans, synonymous with the destruction of a storied American city.

The drowning of that city, the stories of death and survival, and the daring Coast Guard rescues of people from rooftops played out on national television. Add to these storylines the embarrassment and outrage of the incompetence of local, state and federal governments to help American citizens in a timely matter and you have a drama that overshadowed the equally heartbreaking scenes of loss in Mississippi.

Watching from her home in San Antonio, Long Beach native Suzie Kempf was frustrated with the lack of coverage Mississippi received.

"There was such a void of information about Mississippi, my hometown, hundreds of thousands of people, my family and friends," Kempf says. "I literally had dozens of e-mails every day from friends and people I grew up with, trying to get information about people we knew. I heard later of family and friends who waited days for help."

Dick Dickens, also of Long Beach, also believes Mississippi didn't receive the attention it warranted.

"Absolutely, you bet," he says. "You say Long Beach, Mississippi, and nobody knows where that is, but everybody knows New Orleans."

As it was in real time a year ago, the eye of media coverage commemorating the first anniversary will be centered on New Orleans.

But the calamitous assault that Katrina dished out on Mississippi must not be forgotten.

Just some of the numbers give a glimpse of the damage left in Katrina's wake, the most important number being the 231 people the hurricane killed in Mississippi. Eighteen people still are missing and presumed dead.

More than 64,000 homes were destroyed and more than 77,000 were damaged.

The damage or destruction of 13 casinos, critical to Mississippi's economy, cost the state more than $400,000 a day in state tax revenue and affected 17,000 jobs.

In Long Beach, what used to be neighborhoods are now empty lots. One, at the corner of Cleveland Avenue and Fifth Street, is less empty. A red sign put there by Dick and Nola Dickens announces, "We're baack smaller n poorer."

With help from volunteers, the Dickenses have made significant progress rebuilding the house of 21 years that Katrina destroyed.

"She was no lady," Dick Dickens says of Katrina.

The early reincarnation of their new home is the only house on the street. Throughout the area, clothing, plastic bags and paper are ensnared in tree branches, hanging from them, as they have for a year, like ghosts and goblins. Down the street from the Dickenses' house, a black Dell desktop computer dangles from a cedar tree.

Then there are the steps going nowhere.

The steps on Fifth Street, across from the Dickenses, that used to lead into the office of Dr. Ben Kitchings. The steps on Cleveland Avenue that once went into a McDonald's restaurant. The steps on Jeff Davis Avenue that welcomed the faithful of First Baptist Church. The steps on South Burke Avenue that once carried a family into their house.

Steps with nowhere to go after Katrina blew away their destination.

Family surrounded by past
as they build a future

....

GULFPORT, MISS., 8/29/2006

More than 60 years of memories are stacked 30 feet high on the side of the street ready to be picked up. A stranger would call it rubble. A family called it home.

"I see a couple of the babies' toys and carpet I was about to lay down," said 55-year-old Hazel Conner, standing in the hot Mississippi sun, her eyes running up and down the—what, trash? Garbage? Refuse? These are harsh words to describe what was one family's legacy of labor and love. They dishonor the remembrances of things past.

With no respect for history or tradition, Hurricane Katrina, one year ago today, roared across the Gulf Coast and transformed homes into memories.

The white frame, three-bedroom house that sat on about half an acre at 1114 College St. in East Gulfport was surrounded by pecan, oak and maple trees. The trees remain, but the house is a mountain of broken wood and twisted metal waiting to be taken to the dump.

"My daddy and uncle built that house," said Conner, the youngest of five children. At the back of the property can be seen a wall that was part of a motel owned and operated by her family.

Before integration, artists like B.B. King and Bobby "Blue" Bland would stay at the Conner Motel when in town to perform.

Sitting back on the property now are Conner's mobile home and the trailer of her niece, April Moore. Both the mobile home and the trailer were provided by FEMA.

Moore is 25 years old with a 7-year-old daughter, Tá Te Anna, and is pregnant with twins. Katrina blew her life off a track she's struggling to get back on. Before Katrina, Moore lived with her husband and daughter in a comfortable two-bedroom apartment.

"I was going to school and working. I had two cars," she said.

When Katrina struck she heard "the wind gushing and the metal part of the roof flapping against the railing and people screaming 'Oh my God! Oh my God!' "

She remembers the Mississippi rapper, David Banner, coming by and giving away everything he had, including the shoes off his feet.

"He did something," Moore said admiringly.

Having nowhere else to go, she and her family stayed in their apartment, even though it had no electricity or water, until October, when the National Guard forced them to leave.

For a while they lived in a tent on her aunt's property. Later her aunt, in the hospital for congestive heart failure, insisted that Moore and her family sleep in her hospital room, which they did until FEMA gave them a trailer.

The one-bedroom trailer is small, with a tiny bathroom and bathtub not built for a pregnant woman. It's clean and smells of the pork chops that Moore cooks for her husband when he comes home from lunch from his construction job.

They'd like to get a mobile home like her aunt's before the twins arrive in October because there won't be enough room in the trailer for the babies and all that they'll need.

Inside Conner's mobile home, filled with the aroma of a pot of red beans simmering on the stove, Conner looks through a family album of pictures taken inside and outside the destroyed house.

There are old black-and-whites of her parents and of her as a child. There are color photos of Moore, who grew up in the house, taken in the living room or outside by the swings.

Every day she sees what's left of that house. "It's still sad," she said.

One year after Katrina, she's hoping things will get better, because it "can't get much worse."

Next to their property are five trailers belonging to the Presbytery of Mississippi Disaster Recovery who, Conner said, have been "wonderful. They came from all over the country to help."

While she was in the hospital last June, undergoing her second open-heart surgery, the volunteers tore down what was left of her house. The city has yet to pick up the remains.

A white trailer and white mobile home, looking out of place, sit deep in a yard that once nurtured a white house. It was a house that hosted decades of birthday parties, that teemed with the ghosts of Christmases past and in which generations of babies were born.

It's now on the side of the street waiting to be carried away for good.

"We're blessed," said Conner. "Because a lot of people lost their lives, but we're here."

Hiding more than eggs on Easter

3/26/2005

Many, many, many years ago, before the advent of Peeps and Cadbury Eggs, a pair of public relations men who also were devotees of Easter got together to make the holiday at least as big as Christmas. Here's what happened:

"We've got to make Easter big."

"Yes, big!"

"As much a part of the culture as Christmas and Santa Claus is."

"Yes, big!"

"OK, what will best capture the importance of this solemn yet glorious holiday and symbolize the death and resurrection of our Lord Savior?"

"A bunny rabbit!"

"A bunny rabbit?"

"Yeah, yeah, but not just any bunny rabbit. A giant bunny rabbit!"

"A giant bunny rabbit?"

"Yeah, a giant upright bunny rabbit!"

"And what will we name this giant upright bunny rabbit?"

"The Easter Bunny!"

"Why not the Easter Rabbit?"

"Because I have trouble with Rs. It's got to be the Easter Bunny!"

"And what will the Easter Bunny bring?"

"Baskets of candy and some little chicks!"

"Little women? What in the name of Louisa May Alcott are you talking about?"

"No, no. Little baby chickens!"

"What's a giant upright Easter Bunny doing with baby chickens?"

"Doesn't matter!"

"Now, for Christmas we give children gifts. Do we also give them gifts for Easter?"

"Yes, of course!"

"What do we give them? Toys? Clothes? Money?"

"Eggs!"

"What?"

"We give the kids eggs!"

"But the children will break all of these raw eggs and there will be a mess."

"We boil them!"

"The children?"

"No, the eggs! We boil the eggs and give them to the kids!"

"That doesn't seem like much of a present to give a child on Easter, plain white hard-boiled eggs."

"We'll color the eggs!"

"Color the eggs?"

"Yeah, color them pastel colors and make them look real pretty!"

"OK. So we have these pretty colored hard-boiled eggs that will be Easter gifts for children. How do we give it to them? Do we gift-wrap them, leave them in their rooms for them to find when they wake up, or do we just give them the eggs?"

"No, no, no! We hide them!"

"Hide the eggs?"

"Yeah, yeah, yeah! We hide the eggs!"

"So these colored hard-boiled eggs that we're giving the children we're actually not going to give them but we're going to hide them from the children and make them work for it?"

"Yeah, yeah! We make the little thumb suckers run around like crazy looking for them!"

"Well, I guess the only thing we need to do is decide on an annual date for Easter."

"No date!"

"What do you mean, no date! People know that Dec. 25 is Christmas and that Feb. 14 is Valentine's Day. Easter needs its own date."

"No date!"

"Then how about the fourth Sunday in March or the second Sunday in April?"

"No, no! We want people to go into every year not sure when Easter will be!"

"So it's like the eggs?"

"Yeah, yeah! We hide Easter!"

Man from Springfield
a colossal individual

SPRINGFIELD, ILL., 2/13/2007

Who's buried in Lincoln's tomb?

Sitting on more than 12 elevated acres, the 117-foot-tall granite tomb overlooks the oak trees and winding roads of the Oak Ridge Cemetery, whose grounds, on this Sunday, are a checkerboard of grass and old snow. Inside the burial room of polished marble are the vaults of Mary Todd Lincoln, three of the four Lincoln sons and Abraham Lincoln himself.

Who is Lincoln? This is the question the nation was asking about the then-president-elect when he departed from Springfield for Washington on Feb. 11, 1861, to take his oath of office. A statue of Lincoln stands atop the tomb and faces south where, just a few miles away, stands the brown, two-story house at Eighth and Jefferson streets where he lived. Inside the house is the staircase handrail Lincoln would have grasped as he walked down the stairs, out of the house, toward the train depot and to his destiny on that February morning, one day before his 52nd birthday.

In a tearful farewell at the depot, Lincoln said, "Here I have lived a quarter of a century, and have passed from a young to an old man. Here my children have been born, and one is buried. I now leave, not knowing when, or whether ever, I may return, with a task before me greater than that which rested upon Washington."

He would not return to Springfield alive. But in little more than four years he was transformed from a relatively obscure prairie lawyer into an iconic figure. It's said that more books have been written about Lincoln than any other person in history, with the possible exception of Christ.

Still, in some ways he remains elusive to us, this brooding yet funny, idealistic yet pragmatic, homespun but literary, visionary yet haunted genius.

He was our greatest and most indispensable president. He may have sounded presumptuous when he claimed that the task ahead of him was greater than that of Washington, but he was right. Washington was in charge of an infant nation coming together. Lincoln was taking the reins of a young nation falling apart.

Whether or not Lincoln became president, we would eventually have had a Civil War. Four million slaves guaranteed that. For all that the Founding Fathers did right, their most morally inexcusable and tragic mistake was in not abolishing the institution of slavery and in not letting the bell of liberty ring also for their black countrymen and women on July 4, 1776. Many of the founders were influenced by the British political philosopher John Locke but ignored his warning that when you make a man your slave you enter into a state of war with him. The Civil War was a manifestation of that dynamic. And for all his wartime mistakes, who better than Lincoln to lead the nation in such a war? The Democrat he beat for the presidency, Stephen Douglas, would have prolonged the agony of slavery and been a mere stopgap for an inevitable war. (He wasn't even the greatest Douglas of his era; that honor belonged to Frederick Douglass.)

Too much time is spent debating whether Lincoln was a racist, but in the context of his times his views on race were liberal and even those comments of his that give rise to the question were often made when it would have been political suicide to be more liberal. Lincoln the politician understood that sails had to be trimmed if he were to become Lincoln the statesman guiding the ship of state. But consistent in his speeches before and after his election as president is his hatred of slavery and his passionate belief in slaves' humanity.

Lincoln, one of our greatest writers, was a linguistic general who marshaled the power of language to speak to the better angels of our nature while casting out the demons so that we could have a new birth of freedom.

Who's buried in Lincoln's tomb? A man whose departure from Springfield saved a nation and carried him to immortality.

Obama's blackness irrelevant

8/14/2007

Were Barack Obama an exciting new recording artist, would anyone be reluctant to buy his CD out of concern that he wasn't black enough? Were he a talented wide receiver in the NFL draft, is there a general manager who wouldn't pick him because he may not be black enough? If he were a new doctor in town, would a prospective patient be concerned if he was black enough?

When Obama, the freshman senator from Illinois and Democratic candidate for president, is introduced before speeches, he's come onto the stage to songs such as Curtis Mayfield's "Keep On Pushing" and Jackie Wilson's "(Your Love Has Lifted Me) Higher and Higher." It would be understood, however, if he changed his campaign theme song to the 1973 Billy Paul song "Am I Black Enough for You?" because, apparently for some voters—particularly black voters—the answer is no.

Every presidential candidate must answer questions that are particular to them and their life stories. When Obama answers questions about his youth and experience, or lack of experience, people can judge him by how well he answers the questions. But how can he answer the ridiculous and insulting question, "Is he black enough?"

It's a question that's been shadowing him since last year, most recently in a forum at last week's annual convention of the National Association of Black Journalists and, last month, in a *Newsweek* cover story. It's a question that wouldn't be asked if Obama wasn't the child of a white mother and Kenyan father.

That his heritage and background are different from most African Americans led some to question his "blackness," even though it's a heritage that ties him directly to Africa, meaning

Obama can visit his kinfolk in the Motherland. How many of his blacker-than-thou critics can say the same?

Asking if he's black enough assumes that there's a template for being black and a narrow and particular way in which black people are supposed to think, talk and act. It denies the reality that African Americans are as diverse as any other community.

No one asks if Hillary is woman enough or if Edwards is Southern enough or if Rudy is Italian enough; to ask such questions would be as foolish as asking if someone is black enough.

This gets at something that's beyond Obama and race: the question of who has a right to define anyone's identity. Whether it's nationality, religion, ethnicity, politics or any social group, there are always people who will be accused of not being authentic enough or out of lockstep with the program to be "(fill in the blank) enough."

There are always arrogant gatekeepers who presume to possess the power and authority to grant or deny access into the halls of authenticity.

And just what is the barometer for deciding if anyone is black enough to be president? Which one of our many black presidents of the United States set the bar so high for Obama? You know that whole Toni Morrison thing about Bill Clinton being our first black president? She's a writer, y'all.

Depending on one's politics or positions on any given issue, there are good reasons to vote for Obama and good reasons not to vote for him; reasons more rational and substantial than whether he's "black enough."

Maybe those who will vote in the presidential primaries and have reached the conclusion that Obama isn't black enough for them can share with us which candidates, among those running, are black enough to get their vote.

Is it Tom Tancredo or Dennis Kucinich?

Remembering beloved Kendra

9/14/1994

Purple was her favorite color. So at the memorial service in Gonzales, Texas, commemorating the one-year anniversary of her death, the program was purple.

Family and friends wore purple ribbons. The candle her parents lit was in a purple vase with a large purple bow. The large wreath that would later be placed on her grave was purple.

On Sept. 2, 1993, Kendra Lea Clack was raped and strangled in her home. She was 19. The case remains unsolved.

Gonzales, 62 miles east of San Antonio, was the site of the first shots fired in the Texas Revolution. It's also famous for its sausage and the poultry and eggs it produces. Its small-town intimacy is evident on Friday nights in the fall as the community of 7,200 comes together to cheer on the Gonzales Apaches football team.

Until her graduation in 1992, Kendra was a cheerleader for Gonzales High. She was "the base," one of those who provides the foundation and strength for the pyramids and routines. Everyone knew her. Almost everyone loved her.

Such was the breadth of her popularity and the depth of feelings she inspired that more than 500 people, black, white and brown, attended her Labor Day funeral. It was standing room only. Dozens of mourners unable to get in the church stood outside in the heat. When she was 14, Kendra wrote a poem in which she asked God to keep the twinkle in her eyes. He did. She was smart, with beauty queen looks and an angel's heart, but it was her eyes dancing with laughter and life that first drew you to her.

One year after they were prematurely closed, the twinkling

eyes continue to haunt and enchant those who loved her as they live with the joy of her memory and the pain of her absence.

This month her family and friends gathered to remember the girl with the twinkling eyes. Through tears and smiles, stories were told of Kendra the dedicated Sunday school secretary. Kendra, a voice of reason at a time of racial tension in high school. Kendra, the independent college student who wanted to work with children. Kendra, the true friend offering an ear or words of advice. Kendra, the special daughter and sister. Kendra, the beloved.

The minister spoke words of solace and wisdom, but once he misspoke, saying that Kendra's parents, Martin and Jereline, needed mercy and not justice. They need both. You don't get over losing a child. It's something you bear with all the faith and strength you can summon. They've done this with dignity and grace.

But for Kendra's family and friends, a sense of closure can only be achieved through justice. The unsolved murder of a loved one unleashes a tide of suspicion and theories. Again and again you painfully go over the facts of the crime—your mind balking at graphic details—as if the killer's identity will suddenly be revealed in one of the scenarios. Anyone who ever spoke a cross word to her or cast her an angry glance moves to the top of the list of suspects. The mystery thickens in a small town where, in a vacuum of information about progress in the investigation, rumor and innuendo spread freely.

Then there is that raw and primal desire for retaliation against the sorry punk once he's caught, so strong that an abhorrence against vigilantism and a reverence for nonviolence and rule of law doesn't quell the yearning for five minutes to extract some serious Old Testament revenge. Such feelings can only be pacified when the murderer is arrested and convicted. Justice is needed to punish the guilty and help heal the grieving.

Kendra, forever 19, rests in a cemetery surrounded by people who lived into their seventies and eighties. A large cedar tree stands guard over her grave, offering shade to her many visitors. Some come with flowers and all come with memories, including the cousin, unable to write about her until now, whose favorite one is of a young girl with twinkling eyes and a giggle in her voice playing tag on a summer night.

She was it.

Stand up to racism, Victoria

9/25/2007

"Hi. My name is Victoria. I am 17 years old right now and I'm watching the news and reading some of the news online, and there is something I'm hearing that I would like you to write about and give your opinion on. It's the 'Jena Six.' I heard about what happened and I really don't think it's anywhere near fair. I, myself, do think it has to do with race, and it's just the craziest thing because I was just talking with some friends not too long ago and a question came up, when we were discussing life itself: 'If racism would ever stop?' In my opinion, it could but I don't think it ever will. I think people are always gonna judge you wherever you go and race is going to be one of those judgments."

Dear Victoria: I think thousands of years ago two strangers came upon each other, were frightened at their physical differences and fled from each other. Because they never tried to get to know and understand each other, in their isolation they proceeded to imagine the worst about each other and blame the other for all that went wrong.

We've been fighting their battles ever since.

Jena, La., and the overcharging of six black youths is one of those battles, a reminder of double standards in the meting out of punishment and the dispensing of justice. Duke University and the false rape allegations against three white lacrosse players was one of those battles, allegations given traction and a fast track toward maligning and condemning those players because the accuser was black.

The Jenas and Dukes don't materialize out of a vacuum but are given life by decades and centuries of bad history and mistrust. Even when we move forward and further away from the worst of that history, even when we acknowledge it and try to make amends for it, we find we can't completely discard that awful baggage bequeathed to us by those who preceded us on this planet.

Victoria, you're wise to say that you don't think racism will ever stop because bigotry and hatred are evils and evil is a reality. There will always be those who will cloak the stranger in the garment of their suspicion, shroud them in the overcoat of their fears and shun he who is unfamiliar and she who is unknown.

There will always be those who believe that the greater the distance kept from those who are different, the less likely they'll have to get to know them—and if they don't know them, they can stereotype them and pigeonhole them in the crevices of their ignorance.

But the theme of the civil rights movement wasn't "we shall eliminate" but "we shall overcome." That's why I'm pleased that you think the possibility of racism ending exists, which means you'll at least try to end it because it's only in the trying that it can be overcome, if not eliminated.

Speak out and raise your voice in indignation against injustice in Jena, at Duke and wherever you see it. Just don't let your indignation be selective. Wherever you see wrong, raise your voice against it. It doesn't matter who is committing the wrong or who is being wronged. What matters is that the wrong is being done and that people must raise their voices against it. Also understand that speaking out will sometimes put you at odds with allies and the people whose approval you value the most.

But stand firm in your convictions if that's what you believe.

You're right that there will always be people who judge you unfairly for many reasons, and there's not much you can do about that. As long as you carry yourself in dignity and grace and do what you were put on this earth to do, their judgment of you can never be so low as to trip you up.

I admire your thoughtfulness and passion and am given fresh

hope that you and your friends care so deeply about the world and your place in it.

Dr. King once said that we're not where we ought to be but thank God we're not where we used to be. Your generation, like each generation before you, has the opportunity to take us closer to where we ought to be.

Peace and good luck.

Name it, I've been called that

4/3/2008

I was sitting in my office, listening to Jim Croce's "I've Got a Name" and opening a vein in my arm to draw blood so that I could later buy a couple of gallons of gas when Bosswoman's secretary tapped on the cage door.

"Clyde," she said. "BW wants to see you."

"Great," I answered. "By the way, it's Cary."

"Who?"

"Me."

"Clyde?"

"No, Cary."

"Whatever."

I'm a favorite of Bosswoman, who sees me as a son or a brother or a stepmother's godson nine times removed. As I walked in, I reflected on how my visits to her office are the highlights of her day, giving her a few minutes with one of her favorite people in the world.

"I don't know who you are, but get out of my office now!"

Then again, I do have that effect on people.

"BW, it's me," I said.

"Who?"

"Me, Cary."

"Clyde?"

"No, Cary."

"Cary who?"

"Clack."

"Clark?"

"No," I said. "Clack."

"Then who's Clark?" she asked.

"I don't know, but my name is Cary Clack."

"What in the heck is a Cary Clack?"

"Me."

"Whatever. Listen Clark, I'm pleased to announce that you've been chosen the Employee of the Month."

"I won! I won! It took me 13 years, but I won! You must really, really like me!"

"Not so much, Kenny. It was a process of elimination. You were the only employee who hadn't won. It was a close vote, but we didn't think it would be right to choose the intern we hired on Monday over you."

"Thanks."

"But if she'd been here for a week she would have kicked your behind."

"Does the award come with a prize?" I asked. "Can you hook a brother up with a full tank of gas?"

"No, Kevin, but here's a nice certificate."

"Ma'am, this certificate has me listed as Gary."

"And what a fine, fine name Gary is," she said.

"Yes, if your name is Gary. My name is Cary with a 'C' not a 'G'! My name is Cary. It's not Gary. It's not Clyde or Kenny or Kevin. I'm not an animal! I am a human being! I—am—a man!"

"What?"

"I'm sorry," I said. "I saw *The Elephant Man* last night and got carried away. But my name is Cary, as in Cary Grant."

"Wow!" Bosswoman said. "You were named after a movie star? Cary Grant?"

Bosswoman took the certificate from my hands and called out to her secretary. When she came in, Bosswoman handed her the certificate.

"Here, we made a mistake. We have Clyde's name wrongly listed as Gary, but he was named after the movie star, so have it changed to Clark Grant, our newest Employee of the Month."

Coretta's march

Of all the bouquets of flowers that have been given to Coretta Scott King since her death, the most precious were offered in the rain and the cold just after midnight Tuesday. As the motorcade carrying her casket left Ebenezer Baptist Church, where more than 40,000 people had paid their respects for the viewing, two homeless men tossed roses at it.

Sometimes the simplest gestures make for the grandest tributes.

Later Tuesday, in the 10,000-seat New Birth Missionary Baptist Church, presidents, senators, congressmen, foreign leaders, entertainers and others who are called dignitaries gave Mrs. King a rousing and glorious home-going service.

But the marching feet of a few thousand men and women for whom there was no room in that sanctuary said just as much, if not more, about the meaning of Mrs. King's life and work. It was an unplanned and unscripted act that was both symbolic and substantive.

Call it the "march on new birth," or simply "Coretta's march."

People who wanted to attend the funeral had to gather at the Mall at Stone Crest in the Atlanta suburb of Lithonia to catch shuttle buses.

By the time 59-year-old Dee Lee got in line at 8:30 Tuesday morning, thousands of people snaked through the mall parking lot for more than a mile in the near-freezing weather.

Some had been there since 10 o'clock the night before.

"Why would anyone get here at 10 at night?" a woman asked.

"So they could be up there in front instead of back here," Lee answered.

A New Jersey native who now lives in Atlanta, Lee attended the funeral of Martin Luther King Jr.

Looking at the people in the parking lot waiting for the buses to begin loading, she said: "This is us at our finest. This blows my mind. I'm absolutely astounded."

But nearly 2½ hours later, with the cold air and biting wind numbing feet and faces, it was announced that there would be no more bus service because the church and the overflow area were full.

This hurt and angered people, many of whom had traveled from across the country.

"This is unfair," Janice Sims said. "We came to say goodbye and have closure."

By then people had made the decision to march the 3 to 4 miles to the church.

Dressed in their Sunday finest—and clothes and shoes not meant for such a long jaunt—they surprised traffic police and motorists with their procession.

Someone began singing the civil rights song "Ain't Gonna Let Nobody Turn Me Around."

A man coming from the church leaned out a bus window and shouted, "The church is full!"

"That's not the point," a woman shouted back. "We're making a statement and showing our love and respect for Coretta."

Lynette Joyce said, "They gave so much to us. This is the least I can do. I'm in no ways tired."

Seeing two young men, she urged them, "Come on, brothers, march!"

The marchers were black, white and brown, young and old, all joining in their civil and dignified journey.

Some walked with crutches, walkers and canes up the hilly street. Some DeKalb County police officers gave older marchers rides to the church.

"This is the way to do it," said Deidra Johnson, from Bryan, who now lives in Atlanta. "With Rosa, it was the bus; with Martin, it was the march."

Ardell Woodward, in from Washington, said, "This woman means too much to me to turn back now."

As it turned out, the overflow room, which seats more than 2,000 people, was only one-third full.

Some of the marchers, tired and aching, sat down to watch the funeral on the three screens. Others, having made their statement, started the long walk back to the mall and their vehicles.

Four United States presidents came together in New Birth Missionary Baptist Church to give powerful testimony to the life of Coretta Scott King.

But more eloquent was the soft tapping of footsteps on pavement, the footsteps of those who wouldn't be denied the chance to say goodbye to her.

Money talks, not Municipal Courts

11/29/2007

As I begin writing these words on Tuesday afternoon, I have been on the telephone on hold with the City of San Antonio Municipal Courts for 2 hours and 8 minutes. My second wind has kicked in, and I'm feeling exhilarated because I think I may hit three hours. More than 53 years after Roger Bannister ran the first four-minute mile, I have a chance at the Three-Hour Hold, perhaps not a world record but easily a personal best.

My unexpected quest began this afternoon when I received a notice that I had one unpaid parking ticket. Stressing the seriousness of my crime were these boldfaced words: NOTE: THIS VEHICLE IS SUBJECT TO IMPOUNDMENT OR IMMOBILIZATION (mechanical boot) IMMEDIATELY (TRC 682.010). FAILURE TO PAY OR APPEAR MAY RESULT IN REVOCATION (denial) OF YOUR DRIVERS LICENSE OR VEHICLE REGISTRATION.

The boot? For one unpaid parking ticket? I got the ticket on Nov. 9 for an expired parking meter. You have 14 days to pay the fine of $20 before it goes up to $30. I had until Nov. 23 to pay the ticket. By Nov. 24, the date on my notice, I was a scofflaw in the city's eyes, and it was mailed on Monday so that I could get it today. But last week I'd mailed a check to Municipal Courts, so at 1:55 today, Tuesday afternoon, with check number in hand, I called Municipal Courts to explain that. If they hadn't received it, I needed to find out what happened to my check.

After about 20 minutes on hold, I got interested in just how long it would take to talk to someone. After 45 minutes, knowing I had nothing scheduled for the afternoon and some things to busy myself with, I decided I would wait this thing out.

While on hold, I listened to music that is best described as elevator music without the soul. I was told that I could visit any of the Municipal Courts Community Link Service Centers and, approximately every 46.6 seconds (I put the stopwatch on it), a woman's recorded voice assured me, "All attendants are still busy. Please continue holding. Your call will be answered as soon as possible."

After a little more than an hour, realizing I could have driven to Austin in that time, I prepared and ate a meal, brushed and flossed my teeth, washed dishes, put a load of clothes in the washer, wrote in my notebook and listened to Wolf Blitzer boast, again, that CNN has the best political team on TV while I waited for MSNBC's *Hardball* to come on.

At 90 minutes, knowing he's had similar experiences, I e-mailed "Unc," Roddy Stinson, to see what his longest wait was. He replied, "it's God's punishment for writing that letter a couple of weeks ago to bob richter and pretending to be someone else who missed roddy, ken, carlos and ESPECIALLY cary clack. I knew that would boomerang on you. r."

I wrote back and asked when he was retiring.

At a little more than two hours I realized it would have been faster to walk to each of the Community Link Centers to discuss my ticket. At 2½ hours I finished reading the special issue of *Newsweek* about the year 1968. By then I felt as if I'd been on hold since 1968.

With my home phone stuck to my ear I used my cell phone to call neighbors and friends to inform them that I was closing in on three hours. By then, I understood that I wasn't only holding for myself but for all of the people ever put on hold by bureaucracies; all of the people who hung up after 30 or 45 minutes because, unlike me, they have real lives yet wondered just how long they would have had to hold.

At 4:55 I crashed through the Three-Hour Barrier but held on until 5:01 before hanging up. I was on hold for 3 hours, 5 minutes and 17 seconds and had listened to the recording about my call being answered as soon as possible almost 400 times.

I popped open a bottle of eggnog to celebrate my feat of endurance and was full of myself until I remembered that I still had the problem of a supposedly unpaid parking ticket and would have to call again or go there in person.

One suggestion for Municipal Courts: instead of the elevator music for people who are on hold for unconscionable amounts of time, put on a language course instead. At least while we're waiting for service we can learn Italian.

Oh, St. Anthony, hear this fan's plea

1/13/2008

To: St. Anthony of Padua

From: Me

Dear St. Anthony: About a half-hour before kickoff this afternoon, I will don my blue Dallas Cowboys Tony Dorsett jersey, emblazoned with the white No. 33, and put my Cowboys cap on backward in tribute to Tony Romo. But, dear saint, before doing either of those things, to prove that you're my favorite Tony, I will light two of your votive candles.

As a lifelong Cowboys fan born and raised in the city named after you, St. Anthony, I invoke your help as Da Boyz begin their playoff season this afternoon against the New York Giants. You, the patron saint of so many worthwhile causes, are most notably known as the patron saint of lost articles. Which isn't to be confused with St. Jude, the patron saint of lost causes.

A franchise that has been to more Super Bowls than any other in NFL history and is tied for most Super Bowl victories can never be seen as a lost cause. But the last Cowboys team to win a Super Bowl was the team of 1995, and the Boys haven't won a playoff game since December 1996.

The lost articles they and we, their fans, need to recover are three postseason wins and the Lombardi Trophy.

I think it's a blessed coincidence that my city is named after a saint who can be of such help. What if this city had, instead, been named after St. Timothy, the patron saint of stomach problems? How low on the hierarchy of saints do you have to be to get stomach problems as your cause?

But, St. Anthony, if you don't come through for us today, I will be imploring St. Timothy to calm my upset stomach.

St. Anthony, in the name of Jethro Pugh, I ask you to help the Cowboys find their way to the promised land—which this year is Phoenix, the site of Super Bowl XLII.

So much has changed since the Cowboys won that last championship after the 1995 season.

Back then, a Clinton was in the White House and a Bush was preparing to run for president. Now a Bush is in the White House and a Clinton is running for president.

Back then, one of baseball's all-time greats (Pete Rose) was assumed by most people to be lying about doing something wrong. Now two of baseball's all-time greats (Barry Bonds and Roger Clemens) are assumed by most people to be lying about doing something wrong.

That's a long time. By the grace of Roger Staubach, hear my cry.

There has been a lot of silly talk about Tony Romo's romance with Jessica Simpson and the distractions she may pose—and, my, how that girl can pose. If taking a trip to Mexico relaxes Romo and makes him play better, I don't care if he's canoodling with O. J. Simpson.

I don't believe in the Jessica jinx, but if there's anything to it that might put a Cowboys victory in jeopardy, would you use your powers in reverse and make her lose the directions to Texas Stadium?

And if you're not going to help Roy Williams find the talent he's lost, could you see that he loses his way to the game, too?

St. Anthony, I know there are far more important things I should be asking of you. But I can't think of a single one right now. I'm just asking that you do the wonderful things you do.

Oh, and one more request: T. O.'s ankle. I couldn't find a patron saint for temperamental but extraordinarily talented wide receivers with a high-ankle sprain. However, I do see that St. Rocco, a 14th-century Frenchman, is the patron saint of knee problems. Knee. Ankle. Hey, close enough. Could you put in a word for us and tell him to take care of our player's ankle?

And tell him that for more than 80 years, Aliquippa, Pa., has celebrated the Feast of St. Rocco. And Aliquippa is the hometown of Tony Dorsett.

Listen! They're playing their song

2/10/2008

As a veteran of a few dance floors, I've seen a lot of sad things over the years.

There's the couple taking dance lessons who practice their newly learned moves in clubs even though those moves don't go with the song, who find nothing wrong with doing the tango to KC and the Sunshine Band's "I'm Your Boogie Man."

There's the man who dances as if he's trying to hail a taxi and fend off a swarm of bees at the same time but, God love him, thinks he moves like Usher and is having the time of his life.

And there are those like me who, when the Commodores sing "Brick House"—"Shake it down, shake it down down"—find it increasingly difficult to shake it down and aren't certain we'll be able to shake it back up.

But, by far, the saddest sight is a young man, new to the game, who doesn't know that when "I Will Survive" is played, he shouldn't try to dance with the women filling the dance floor.

So this column is a public service announcement to young men across the nation: As soon as you hear the opening chords of "I Will Survive," run—do not walk—off the dance floor, or you will be trampled and sacrificed to the gods of bad relationships.

Released in 1978, "I Will Survive" is No. 489 on *Rolling Stone* magazine's list of the 500 greatest songs of all time. Sung by Gloria Gaynor, it's one of the best songs of the disco era, a song so irresistible that Egyptian mummies have been recorded nodding their heads and tapping their feet to it.

But because the song is about a woman who survived an awful relationship with a lying, cheating, no-good scoundrel and is now triumphant in her strength and independence, it is also one of the all-time great empowerment songs for women.

Which is why, when that song is played, women rush to the floor and engage in a euphoric, affirming and cleansing tribal dance in which they exorcise the demons of bad relationships.

Don't get me wrong. "I Will Survive" isn't an anti-man song. But it is an anti-man-at-this-moment-but-I'll-be-all-right-as-soon-as-it's-finished song.

When it begins to play, veterans of dance floors know what to do. Men exit the floor as quickly as they can, order a drink, scan the group of women to see if they've wronged any of them and, if they have, quietly slip out of the club. The couple taking dance lessons will split up; she'll tango by herself among the women while her partner, standing at the bar, counts off her steps.

Young men, do not—I repeat, DO NOT—attempt to join the women on the dance floor during "I Will Survive." This is their song.

Sure, the NFL players in the movie *The Replacements* danced to it, but most of those actors have since been blackballed in Hollywood.

Women not only dance together during this song; they also sing the lyrics as they remind each other that, yes, sisters, we have survived.

Young men, not only do you look silly being the only man dancing to "I Will Survive," but they don't want you there. When they sing the lyrics, "Go on now, go walk out the door, just turn around now, 'cause you're not welcome anymore," they mean it.

And it's about that moment in the song when some of them will have flashbacks, see you, think you're the man, or men, who dogged them out, inform the other women and, just like that, all that pent-up fury and bad memories are directed at you.

I once saw a guy on a dance floor in Atlanta disappear amid a group of women during "I Will Survive." He was never seen again. I know of another guy in Houston who thought he would dance with the women during that song, and they turned on him. He made it out alive, but to this day he is an emotional wreck. Whenever he hears "I Will Survive," he falls to the floor in a fetal position, sobs uncontrollably and mumbles, "I'm sorry, please forgive me."

All I'm saying, young bloods, is that if you try to infiltrate the empowering group sisterhood of dance during "I Will Survive," you may not survive.

It's a great song, but it's not your song; it's theirs. Wait it out, let the song end, applaud when they come off the floor and then ask one of them to dance to "My Girl."

President should've asked us for more

1/21/2007

The president of the United States is giving me more credit than I deserve. He has looked into my soul and seen a valor that lies dormant. He has reviewed my conduct of the past four years and saluted accomplishments that don't exist. He has praised a commitment to something greater than me that hasn't been tested— indeed, that he hasn't asked to be tested.

Yes, the president is much too kind and generous and saying graciously abundant things about me that I would be rightly embarrassed to say about myself.

Perhaps you saw him because he was equally extravagant about you. Last week on PBS' *NewsHour*, Jim Lehrer asked President Bush why, if the war in Iraq is so important, he hadn't asked more Americans to sacrifice something.

The president responded by saying, "I think a lot of people are in this fight. I mean, they—they sacrifice peace of mind when they see the terrible violence on TV every night. I mean, we got a fantastic economy here in the United States but yet, when you think about the psychology of the country, it is—it is somewhat down because of the war."

That's why I must deflect the president's compliments and return his bouquet of thanks. Maybe I'm just too humble and unable to comprehend all that I've given, but I can't see how my losing some peace of mind about the war is on a par with a soldier who has lost a piece of her body in the war.

One of the curiosities about this administration's conduct after 9-11 is why more wasn't asked of the American people during the War on Terror and the war in Iraq, specifically, those Americans who weren't in the military or had no family in the military.

When, in his finest and most unscripted moment as the commander in chief, President Bush stood on the rubble of the Twin Towers, took the bullhorn and said those responsible will soon hear from us, he had the support of us all. There is little he could have asked of us that we wouldn't have done in pursuit of—remember this name?—Osama bin Laden.

Instead, he told us to go shopping.

Now, four years into a war that's lost the nation's support, the only Americans still being asked to sacrifice anything are the troops and their families. Such is the character and heart of this nation that even in an unpopular war in which we seem powerless to prevent the killings of more American soldiers and Iraqi citizens, a sense of justice informs us that it's not right for only those who wear the uniform to bear the cost.

Having our peace of mind disturbed is a consequence of living, an everyday reality. There will always be events that roil the serene waters of our peace of mind. A mother throwing her children into the San Francisco Bay, crime in our cities, problems at work or at home bother our peace of mind.

But a war is an extraordinary event in the life of a nation, and a nation of 300 million people could do more to make the burden less onerous for those in battle. For most of us, it's easy to turn off the war and pretend it's not happening. Peace of mind? A sacrifice?

Not when there are 20-year-olds suffering from burns over 75 percent of their bodies who have won Purple Hearts they'll never be able to hold; not when there are families with permanent absences at their dinner tables; not when there are members of the National Guard and reservists spending three or four tours while their families back home buckle under financial stress; not when thousands more are being sent into the maw of Iraq while the rest of us look forward to the Presidents Day sales.

Mr. President, I appreciate your appreciation of my great sacrifice of my peace of mind but, believe me, there was nothing to it.

Great joy can turn a city into a family

6/16/2003

All day Sunday, the city waited for the Moment.

All day it loomed, like the rain clouds that sometimes seemed close enough to touch, rain clouds that threatened to open up at any minute.

All day, fans prepared themselves for the Moment, looking ahead with anticipation before reining it in, not wanting to get too far ahead of themselves.

The Moment would come sometime that night in the SBC Center, when the final buzzer of the NBA season would sound, proclaiming the San Antonio Spurs the new world champions and unleashing a wave of ecstasy that would wash over all of San Antonio.

The rain clouds never released their pent-up storm, and for a while Sunday night it appeared as if the Moment of frenzied celebration would be denied Spurs fans.

But at approximately 10:18, the Moment, sweet and delicious, was delivered and a silver-and-black dream came true.

Sunday night was one of those private and public nights in our lives we never want to end: moments of magic we want to savor until they're forever preserved in memory.

The unbridled joy, the laughing, yelling, high-fives and joyous jumping and running of Spurs fans will not soon be forgotten.

Along Commerce Street, residents stood outside their homes holding signs, cheering and waving to motorists who answered them with the most harmonious blaring horns heard here since 1999, the last time the Spurs won the title.

Two little girls who sat holding signs in their front yard at

Commerce and Polaris streets before the game now jumped around, one blowing a toy horn.

On the corner of Hackberry and Nolan, three young men shouted, "We did it! We did it!"

Enjoy this. Not just the joy of being the best basketball team on earth but the bonding, however fleeting, of San Antonians.

Except in an extraordinary time of tragedy, a community is never as close as it is when celebrating the championship run of its team.

The night was made sweeter by the final game of David Robinson, a storybook finish to a fabled career.

That Robinson's final game would be on the East Side was just, for it was on the East Side, playing in the Alamodome, that he established his legend and earned his fortune.

And it was from the East Side and to the East Side that he demonstrated a gift for humanity that exceeded his basketball talent.

On Sunday night on Morningview Street, two women and a man shouted "Spurs number one!" near Gates Elementary, the school where Robinson, since 1991, has promised fifth-graders scholarship money if they graduate from high school.

And while Commerce Street was transformed into a loud and joyful party, just off it, in silence and protected by a lone security guard, sat Robinson's greatest gift to this city: the Carver Academy.

Enjoy this, remember this, for the Moment will end.

Nights can't live forever, but a legacy can.

Get there one chat at a time

A perennial rite of road trips is the impatient child in the back seat asking, "Are we there yet?" So eager is she to get to a destination that, for her, it is more of an idea than an actual place.

For centuries, this nation, burdened by the baggage of suspicion and stereotype, has been on a road trip toward racial reconciliation.

Long and difficult, this journey has gone through locales that include Jamestown, Philadelphia, Gettysburg, Chicago, Montgomery, Birmingham, Selma, Boston and Washington, D.C.

It has had drivers, some with a clearer sense of direction than others, who struggled with what routes to take; drivers named Jefferson, Lincoln, Douglass, Sojourner Truth, MLK and LBJ.

And because every trip needs a good book, especially one that attempts to explain where you're going, there have been chroniclers such as Harriet Beecher Stowe, William Faulkner, Ralph Ellison, John Howard Griffin, James Baldwin and Toni Morrison.

And after all these years, all these places, drivers and books, we glance out the window of the passing social landscape, measure the distance traveled and how much farther we need to go, and we ask not only "Are we there yet?" but also "Will we ever get there?"

The journey could never be anything but a bumpy one, filled with detours and roadblocks. But whenever we see an avenue that may make it easier to travel, we should try to take it.

Once a year, it seems, we hit cultural checkpoints where somebody says or does something racial and controversial that causes pundits, academics and social scientists to declare that it's time for a national conversation on race. The conversation lasts for a few paragraphs, drifts off into other topics and is forgotten until the next time someone says something racial and controversial.

This year's presidential campaign has brought us to one of these checkpoints, and such moments are valuable if used correctly. We're obsessed with race yet uncomfortable with talking candidly about it. We are a nation of shadow-boxers sparring with images and reflections and avoiding contact with what is real.

One way to engage with something real and substantive is to talk with those whose differences make us uncomfortable. And while a "national conversation" is fine, the best and potentially most fruitful conversations are those between individuals over the back fence, at work, during lunch, over beers at a bar or on softball fields and in bowling alleys.

These should be conversations that are unflinchingly honest but fueled more by reflection than recriminations; conversations between open minds that acknowledge each other's pain, fears and grievances but that are dedicated to not being shackled by them; conversations in which we hear things we don't want to hear; conversations that are in the spirit of Marvin Gaye when he sang, "Talk to me, so you can see what's going on."

And they should be conversations that don't require anyone to have to "transcend race" or become "colorblind."

When you say someone transcends race, you're saying they weren't good enough for you when you saw them only as black, white or brown. But now that you see that they're not as different from you, they're OK.

Do the patches of a quilt "transcend" cloth? Are they not unique parts of a wonderful and colorful tapestry?

Can a person who is colorblind appreciate the different colors of a rainbow and how they beautifully complement each other?

No one should have to forfeit his or her identity to be accepted or understood.

On Tuesday, I received an e-mail from a reader named Jack that began this way: "Mr. Clack. As a 79-year-old white man who grew up in the North, isolated from black people, I only knew there were 'negroes,' mulattos and whites. Twenty-five years in the Air Force changed nothing; the terms were still the same. After I retired came the terms 'black,' 'African American,' etc. As one whose heritage includes both the black and white world, I wonder if you could do a piece on WHO IS BLACK, or WHAT IS BLACK. Are you, Tony Parker, Tiger Woods and many others of mixed blood considered to be black? Of course, it should not matter what the color of a person's skin is, only their attributes, good and bad. Thank you for any consideration you may give my thoughts."

It's a question asked honestly and with sincerity; a question that shows me that at the age of 79, Jack wants to continue on this journey to reconciliation; a question that can lead to more and tougher questions as well as a spirited but healthy conversation. So I'm giving Jack a call. It won't matter whether the nation has another truncated national conversation. I'm going to have a conversation with Jack.

Something turned boy to killer

10/12/1994

The telephone pole by the creepy two-story house on the corner, going uphill, was one end zone.

The telephone pole by Rev. Black's driveway, going downhill, was the other end zone. Our football field consisted of about 50 yards of the street we lived on.

During our pre-teen and teen years in the 1970s we played hundreds of touch football games on this "field," getting narcissistic kicks at the way the uphill and downhill running developed our leg muscles. We also played tackle in one of our yards. Dino had the best backyard because of its spaciousness. Of all of us, Dino was the slowest runner, but he was quick and had the best arm. He was also the superior basketball player.

As we got older our games decreased and eventually stopped as our athletic activities were restricted to our high school teams. We weren't carefree and innocent, but we were boys sharing camaraderie and fun in a time of infinite possibility and imagination.

What didn't seem possible then was that some of us would fall victims to drug abuse and gang violence. And what didn't seem imaginable was what Dino would do and what that act would do to him.

"Dino" was the nickname of Walter Williams. Shortly after midnight on Oct. 5 he was executed by the state of Texas for the 1981 murder of a convenience store clerk named Daniel Liepold. It took six minutes for him to die.

Capital punishment is wrong for two reasons. For one thing it is racially biased. Historically, studies have shown that blacks are more likely to be executed than whites. Even more insidious is that a murderer is more likely to be sentenced to death if the

199

victim was white rather than black. Most importantly, capital punishment is immoral. No person or state has the right to take another life in the name of justice. One of the purposes of law is to protect us from our passions, such as revenge, while still punishing the guilty in an appropriate manner. Humans have the power to mete out such punishment. Only God has the power to decide who dies.

This isn't to absolve Williams of what he did. He committed a horrible crime that has caused interminable pain to the Liepold family. But does his death make anything better?

Williams' execution made CNN and National Public Radio. A few years ago he was listed in *Ebony* magazine as one of the blacks on death row. It's not the kind of recognition he dreamed of as a boy, yet now his name is forever linked with murder.

But he wasn't a natural born killer, some cinematic villain thirsting for blood. Nothing he did while growing up ever hinted darkly at violence. As the news spread last Tuesday that Williams would die at midnight, neighbors and friends asked themselves and each other the question they've been asking for almost 14 years: "What happened?"

What happened to this young man who'd always been polite, generous, intelligent, articulate and soft-spoken—qualities that led you to believe he would be a success in life?

Abandoned as a baby, Williams was adopted by an older couple (both are now dead). They were nice people, but they may have lacked the energy and discipline to guide him away from bad influences. Part of Williams' problem was that he was too impressionable and too much of a follower. Once he got mixed up with the wrong crowd, he stayed mixed up.

The last time I saw him he drove by my house. In the car with him were some of his new friends. By then he'd begun messing with drugs. He nodded at me, and I nodded back. Trying to act thuggish, he looked like someone trying to act thuggish. It was a pose he would carry out to its tragic conclusion when, sometime after that, he walked into a convenience store with a .38 in his hand.

This isn't an apology for a brutal crime. Nor is it a liberal lament for a confessed murderer. It's just a memory of a friend who was lost and now, through the grace of Allah, may have been found.

Remember this: Before there was the killer, there was the boy.

Paws-ing to savor my links to "Papa"

2/28/2008

I've been an Ernest Hemingway fan for all of my adult life and am always amazed at our similarities.

Hemingway wrote *The Old Man and the Sea*. I hope to one day be an old man who can see. Hemingway once lived in Paris. This past weekend, I walked on Paris Street in Castroville.

Hemingway had a contentious relationship with F. Scott Fitzgerald. I have a contentious relationship with Fitzgerald, who has refused to talk to me since his death in 1940.

Hemingway has a volume titled *The Complete Short Stories of Ernest Hemingway*. I'm working on a volume titled *The Uncompleted Short Stories of Cary Clack*, consisting of short stories that I never finished.

But the main thing I have in common with "Papa" is the white, 6-month-old kitten with six toes named Oops that is, at this moment, nibbling on my feet. Like Hemingway, I have cats that are freaks.

Normal cats have 18 toes, five on each of their front paws and four on each of their back paws. Abnormal cats, called polydactyls, have at least six toes on each of their front paws and at least one extra on their rear paws. They are also called "mitten cats" because of the size of their paws, a size that suggests they're capable of playing third base for the Atlanta Braves.

Hemingway had a home in Key West, Fla., for the last 30 years of his life. Early on, he admired a six-toed tomcat that belonged to a sea captain. The captain gave the cat to Hemingway, and its descendants, known collectively as the Hemingway cats, continue to live at the Hemingway Home and Museum.

In October 2006, I took two female kittens off my mother's

hands with the goal of giving them away. Even though Hemingway was the persona of machismo, I still didn't think owning two kittens was a manly image so I decided to toughen up the cats with strong masculine names that evoked toughness and power.

The tan-colored one with blue eyes became Sinatra, and the gray, striped one became Raskolnikov (Rasko for short), after the coldblooded killer in Fyodor Dostoevsky's novel *Crime and Punishment*.

I've yet to get rid of the cats, but let me tell you, the names toughened them up like you wouldn't believe. There isn't a curtain in South Texas they can't rip to shreds. Yep, my two baaad female cats with the funky paws. Female cats.

So I was a bit surprised last August when I returned home from a business trip, walked into my closet and saw Rasko nursing two kittens, a black one and a white one.

It seems that Sinatra was a male cat and as randy as his namesake, although obviously not as, eh, endowed as the Chairman of the Board, if you know what I mean, because we didn't see it when we checked in 2006.

A couple of days later the black kitten died. My first reaction was why did it have to be the black kitten?

The white kitten survived and has been given the name of Oops, as in, Oops, I didn't know that your father, who is also your uncle, was a male.

I've tried to pawn it off on others. (Get it? Paw-n. That's a little polydactyl cat humor.) When my colleague Michael O'Rourke wrote about his daughter's cat dying, I confess that my second thought was, "That poor child." My first thought was, "Here's a chance to get rid of Oops." But the O'Rourke household already had plans for a new addition.

So here I am, stuck with three incestuous cats that could each win a National League Gold Glove this season. Sinatra has since been neutered, and Oops is a female. I think.

Losing a beloved
family member in Vandross

7/4/2005

In the two years after Luther Vandross suffered the stroke that silenced his magnificent voice, it wasn't unusual for his fans to periodically ask each other, "What's the latest on Luther?" or "Have you heard how Luther is doing?" or "Do you think he'll sing again?" It was as if they were relatives inquiring about the health of a loved one, family members concerned about Uncle Luther or Cousin Luther.

On Friday evening, as the news came out that Vandross had died at the age of 54, that same sense of familiar affection and care circulated through the grapevine as people asked, "Did you hear about Luther?" or "Is it true? Did Luther die?" or "He couldn't have! Not Luther!"

Within the African American community, Vandross was as beloved a musical icon as ever existed. His transcendent talent was on display for all to appreciate and enjoy, and the diversity across race and age of the audience that saw his last performance here in San Antonio, at the Majestic Theatre in December 2001, was a testament to his wide appeal.

But by the time Vandross had his first crossover Top 10 hit in 1989 with the wedding gem "Here and Now," he already was a superstar in the black community—a community that not only referred to him simply as Luther but also, aware of his constant battle with weight, and depending on if he was winning it, called him Big Luther or Skinny Luther.

After Vandross suffered his stroke on April 16, 2003, Aretha Franklin, Jesse Jackson and nationally syndicated radio person-

204

ality Tom Joyner encouraged daily noon prayer vigils across the nation.

At the time, Joyner told *USA Today*, "Luther feels like family. He's not just an artist who's got a lot of hit records. What African American do you know who doesn't have some Luther in their record collection? Mainstream America doesn't realize how huge Luther is with us."

By the time those who weren't regular listeners of R&B radio had discovered Vandross, no less an authority than Smokey Robinson, in his autobiography, had already proclaimed him one of the greatest soul singers in history.

Smokey was correct, but the genre qualifier of "soul" can be dropped and he'd still be right.

No one sounded like Vandross, and he sounded like no one who came before him. With an amazingly expressive tenor that was threaded with silk and the fervor of gospel music, he was the greatest romantic balladeer of the last quarter-century, using his voice to explore love in all its glorious and heartbreaking dimensions.

A Vandross love song wasn't a boastful "Come here woman and see what I'm going to do to you" come-on. It was a gentlemanly invitation to seduction with the promise that the romance was as important as the passion. It was always class.

Many children have been conceived by the music of Vandross, but many couples have also made up and been married to it.

In 54 years, Vandross lived a wonderful life and left us with dozens of memorable, head-shaking performances.

Still, selfishly, we wish we had more of his years and performances to look forward to. Using the title of his first hit record, once exposed to such virtuosity, it's "Never Too Much."

Thanks, Luther.

Rededicating ourselves
to a more perfect Union

7/4/2006

To be an American is not a talent. It's not a craft or skill discovered and manifested early in life that is honed and mastered so that we perform with pride as others marvel at this singular talent.

We didn't will ourselves into existence or align the stars and our bloodlines in our favor so that we would be born in the United States.

When we say we're proud to be an American it should be with the acknowledgment that everyone should be proud of his or her birthright.

To be an American and enjoy freedoms that come with it is a gift of fortune. It must never be forgotten that, but for the grace of God, Allah, Jehovah or whatever divine or nondivine powers one believes put us here, life could have been less fortunate.

But for forces over which we don't possess the talent to change, instead of enjoying barbecue and baseball today, we could just as easily be the dissident languishing in a Chinese prison, a child soldier forced to take up arms in Uganda or Sri Lanka, or a girl trapped as a sex slave in Pakistan.

Were we them, the Fourth of July would be stripped of all its glory and meaning. At best it would be irrelevant; at worst it would be what Frederick Douglass, in 1852, said it was to the American slave: a day that mocks us with its cruelty.

Because we're not that Chinese dissident, that Ugandan or Sri Lankan child soldier, that Pakistani sex slave or, no longer, that American slave, the Fourth of July is as much about Thanksgiving as is the fourth Thursday of November.

This is a great day for celebration and rededication.

A celebration of the liberties and opportunities that are abundant here, but also a rededication to preserving and expanding them and promising ourselves that we will never retreat from honoring the equality of men and women and the protection of their life, liberty and the pursuit of happiness.

A reminder that while we may never be a "more perfect Union," we can't afford complacency, and that in trying to be perfect we at least become better.

There is no contradiction in loving this country passionately while exercising those freedoms of speech and the right to dissent that are among the reasons we love it so much.

No love for anything or anyone should be so blind as to ignore those flaws, which hurts it and hinders its progress.

Like the French Nobel laureate Albert Camus, writing to an imaginary German friend during World War II, each of us should be able to love our country and still love justice.

Equally shortsighted are those who believe that dissent is treasonous, who wish to narrowly define patriotism and who forget that any critique of policies and where we are as a nation is made out of love and the faith that we can be better.

Abraham Lincoln, the most gifted writer of all our presidents, ended his second inaugural address with an oft-quoted paragraph that can never be repeated enough.

He was speaking to a nation at war with itself, but his words also speak to how we must engage each other and this nation's unfinished work: "With malice toward none; with charity for all; with firmness in the right, as God gives us to see the right, let us strive on to finish the work we are in; to bind up the nation's wounds; to care for him who shall have borne the battle, and for his widow, and his orphan—to do all which may achieve and cherish a just and a lasting peace, among ourselves and with all nations."

Witness to a great American moment

11/6/08

We live to see the things that lie beyond our gaze.

On the afternoon of Oct. 15, 1972, before the second game of the World Series in Cincinnati, Major League Baseball honored Jackie Robinson on the 25th anniversary of his breaking the color line. Only 53 years old but looking older, with diabetes ravaging his body, Robinson, nearly blind and with a cane, stood on the field and spoke of how pleased he was, adding, "but I will be more pleased the day I can look over at the third base line and see a black man as manager."

He died nine days later. In 1975, Frank Robinson became MLB's first black manager. Such a simple aspiration for Jackie: to see the first black manager in baseball.

We live to see the things that lie beyond our gaze, holding on to visions that are faint but possible. Scripture reads that faith is the evidence of things not seen.

The United States of America didn't have to elect a black man as president to affirm my faith in its ideals and ceaseless possibilities.

It didn't have to entrust its future to someone who looks more like me than the other men to whom it has entrusted its future to ensure my love and unyielding devotion.

Still . . . and yet . . . but . . .

Wow!

I was standing in my living room, holding a notebook and phone at 10 p.m. Tuesday when it was announced that Barack Obama had been elected president of the United States. I started crying. I knew I would, but the spontaneity of it surprised me. We live to see things that lie beyond our gaze.

When I was a child and, later, a teenager, I never asked any-one if we would ever see a black president. Whatever cornuco-pia of opportunities were out there, that wasn't one of them. It wasn't only beyond my gaze; it was unable to take root in my imagination.

Yet over the past several days and weeks, at the age of 48, I've found myself incessantly asking people, especially older blacks, the question, "Did you think you'd live to see this?"

I've asked my grandmother, my mother, my father, my uncles, friends and strangers. Without exception, they get a quiet, reflec-tive look in their eyes before saying incredulously, "No."

On Monday and then again on Tuesday, my 88-year-old grand-mother, sensing the history she was close to seeing and gushing like a schoolgirl, asked, "Wouldn't that be something? I never would have imagined."

For several months, I've heard and read the suggestions that blacks supporting Obama by more than 90 percent was evidence of their racism.

First, blacks have been giving the Democratic presidential nominee nine of 10 votes for several elections. That may not be wise, but it's the reality.

Second, blacks have historically and consistently voted for white candidates.

Third, it's not as if Obama is Snoop Dogg. And it's not as if, were Mike Tyson running for president, blacks would be stand-ing in line for hours to vote for him. Obama was president of the *Harvard Law Review*, a constitutional law professor, the author of two best-selling books, one of which is a classic in American memoirs. He may be the best prose stylist among our presidents since Lincoln, and one of the constant criticisms of him is that he's "too cerebral."

There's a difference between voting against someone out of

hatred, stereotypes and prejudice and voting for someone out of pride and the belief that he or she can do a good job.

I know scores of black men and women who have fought for this country, worked hard, broken their backs to provide and educate their children, served their communities and churches, and suffered indignities and humiliations most of us can't imagine, and yet they continue to believe in the greatness and possibilities of this nation and teach their children to do the same.

For the first time in their lives and this country's life, they had the opportunity to vote for an intelligent, talented and engaging black candidate for president, and someone wants to call them racist?

No, baby, no.

And Obama didn't become President-elect Obama without the support of white, Latino, American Indian and Asian American voters. On Tuesday night, I received an e-mail from a friend, Lyndon Nugent, the 41-year-old grandson of Lyndon Johnson: "As I think about that I think about how far we have come in 200 years and how much we have come in just the last 2 years. I think that would make LBJ, MLK, JFK, RFK and so many folks involved in the civil rights movement of the 1950s and 1960s so proud is not that we are about to elect America's first African American President. I think what would make them so proud is that we are about to elect an extremely intelligent and charismatic person to be our leader whose talents were ultimately not suppressed because he is an African American."

My 2-year-old next-door neighbor, Tristan Villafranca, the grandson of Mexican immigrants, says, "Obama is my president."

Obama is our president, even for those who didn't vote for him.

I was in Springfield, Ill., that February day last year when Obama announced his candidacy for president. At the time I wrote, "He's either the baseball hotshot who looks great in spring training but fades once the regular season begins or he's a true phenomenon of rare and enduring talent. The long political season will allow us to see if he can translate his considerable gifts into a compelling candidacy."

Back to Jackie Robinson. On the day he made history in his first game with the Brooklyn Dodgers, San Antonio's John "Mules" Miles, a Negro Leagues star with the Chicago American Giants, was listening to the game on a radio with his teammates.

I once asked Miles his reaction when Robinson took the field.

"He made it!" he said. "Thank God, he made it."

We should always hope that a new president, whoever he or she is, becomes the best president we've ever had because the entire nation benefits from it. Obama now has four years to prove what he can do. He won't be graded on a curve. If he fails, he fails. His potential to disappoint is equal to his potential to succeed.

But for those who never thought they'd live to see this day, to bear witness to this astonishing American moment, there is a feeling leaping from the heart that shouts, "He made it! Thank God, he made it."

Maury Maverick Jr.
guided many "children"

1/29/2003

I met an old man in a typewriter shop.

That's how I always answer the question when I'm asked how I got to the *San Antonio Express-News*.

The old man was Maury Maverick Jr., and we met in 1988 in a now-defunct typewriter shop on Goliad Road. In retrospect, he really wasn't that old.

It was a brief meeting, and five years later he invited me to lunch, learned that I wanted to write and took some of my published pieces to the newspaper's editorial board, which gave me a chance.

Years later I learned from Maury that before recommending me to the board, he did a background check on me with his friend and brother in the fight for social justice, the Rev. Claude Black, who lived across the street from me when I was growing up.

In many ways, the column I wrote earlier this month saluting Maury on his birthday was the column I always knew I would write when he died; the column I write now on a sad and gray Tuesday morning after learning that he has just died at the age of 82.

But knowing he was going into the hospital for serious surgery, I wanted to send him a bouquet while he was alive. After it ran, he wouldn't believe me when I told him that the reaction was overwhelmingly positive and that there were only a couple of negative responses. I never told him about those two negative responses.

Elsewhere in today's paper and for the next few days you will read about Maury's legendary political and legal battles, his courageous stands on unpopular issues and the mantle he carried as one of the most prominent liberal voices of his generation.

So I will save the few lines in this space for the more personal memories.

The generosity Maury showed me and the interest he showed in my career was emblematic of a man who fathered no children of his own but who took a paternal interest in younger people whose lives he influenced.

Just a few of "Maury's children" would include writer Naomi Shihab Nye, attorneys Gerald Goldstein and Lou Linden, businessman Claudius Minor, teacher Jack Elder, *Express-News* staffers Jan Jarboe Russell and John Branch and former staffer Bob Richter.

Some of us, while not looking forward to the day, often thought about what a fun funeral Maury would have. This is a man who has requested a "hootchie-coochie dance" for that day.

It's typical in talking about Maury that this morning, after commiserating over his death, Naomi and I started laughing about the funny phone messages he would leave.

When he called me, he'd pretend to be a deceased local black leader, such as Valmo Bellinger or G.J. Sutton. Or he'd ask, "Kiddo, can you help an old honky out?"

He felt a special debt for Sutton, the first black state legislator from Bexar County, and his wife, Lou Nelle, who succeeded him, because they put him on their staffs so he could write speeches and columns for them and earn the necessary years to receive his state pension.

"Don't tell that story until after I'm gone," he said the day before he entered the hospital.

Now he's gone and there will be plenty of stories told by the many who loved him.

Hey, St. Peter, open the gates! Heaven will never be the same, and neither will those of us who knew Maury Maverick Jr.